First Workshop on Natural Language Interfaces 2020

Online
10 July 2020

ISBN: 978-1-7138-1376-7

Printed from e-media with permission by:

Curran Associates, Inc.
57 Morehouse Lane
Red Hook, NY 12571

Some format issues inherent in the e-media version may also appear in this print version.

Printed with permission by Curran Associates, Inc. (2020)

For permission requests, please contact the Association for Computational Linguistics at the address below.

Association for Computational Linguistics
209 N. Eighth Street
Stroudsburg, Pennsylvania 18360

Phone: 1-570-476-8006
Fax: 1-570-476-0860

acl@aclweb.org

Additional copies of this publication are available from:

Curran Associates, Inc.
57 Morehouse Lane
Red Hook, NY 12571 USA
Phone: 845-758-0400
Fax: 845-758-2633
Email: curran@proceedings.com
Web: www.proceedings.com

ACL 2020

First Workshop on Natural Language Interfaces

Proceedings of the Workshop

July 10, 2020
Online

Introduction

Ahmed Hassan Awadallah, Yu Su, Huan Sun, Wen-tau Yih

Natural language interfaces (NLIs) have been the "holy grail" of human-computer interaction and information search for decades. However, early attempts in building NLIs to databases did not achieve the expected success due to limitations in language understanding capability, extensibility and explainability, among others. The last 5 years have seen a major resurgence of NLIs in the form of virtual assistants, dialogue systems, and semantic parsing and question answering systems. The horizon of NLIs has also been significantly expanding beyond databases to, e.g., knowledge bases, robots, Internet of Things, Web service APIs, and more.

This has been driven by a number of profound revolutions: (1) In the big data era, and as digitalization continues to grow, there is a rapidly growing demand for interfaces that connect users to the ever-expanding data sources, services and devices in the computing world. NLIs represent a very promising technology to accomplish that as they provide users with a unified way to interact with the entire computing world using language, their natural way of communication, and (2) the renaissance and development of deep learning have brought us from rule and feature engineering to a world of neural architecture and data engineering, promising better language understanding, adaptability and scalability. As a result, many commercial systems like Amazon Alexa, Apple Siri, and Microsoft Cortana, as well as academic studies on NLIs to a wide range of backends have emerged in recent years.

Many research communities have been advancing NLI technologies in recent years: NLP and machine learning, data management and databases, programming language, human-machine interaction, among others. This workshop aims to bring together researchers and practitioners from related communities to review the recent advances and revisit the challenges that led to the failure of earlier NLI systems, and discuss what the remaining challenges are and what to expect in the short- and long-term future.

This workshop is featured by a strong, diverse lineup of invited speakers: Monica Lam's research on virtual assistants stems from a programming language perspective and emphasizes openness and privacy, Percy Liang is a leading researcher on natural language interaction and machine learning, and is also leading Microsoft's development of next-generation conversation systems, H V Jagadish is a pioneer on database usability and NLIs to databases, Joyce Chai has made fundamental contributions to human-robot interaction, Luke Zettlemoyer is a world-renowned expert in semantic parsing, question answering, and natural language processing in general, and Imed Zitouni is an industrial leader on conversational AI with decades of experience at IBM, Microsoft, and Google. The program is also featured by many innovative and forward-looking papers that explore different aspects of NLIs, ranging from compositionality to personalization to data to generation to deployment and interactive learning. We warmly welcome everyone to the workshop, and hope you will enjoy the rich program that covers the past, the present, and the future of NLIs from different research communities.

Organizers:

Ahmed Hassan Awadallah, Microsoft Research
Yu Su, The Ohio State University
Huan Sun, The Ohio State University
Wen-tau Yih, Facebook AI Research (FAIR)

Program Committee:

Danqi Chen, Princeton
Li Dong, Microsoft Research Asia
Xinya Du, Cornell
Kevin Duh, Johns Hopkins University
Ahmed Elgohary, University of Maryland
Hao Fang, Microsoft Semantic Machines
He He, New York University
Lifu Huang, UIUC
Srinivasan Iyer, University of Washington
Robin Jia, Stanford
Bernhard Kratzwald, ETH
Jayant Krishnamurthy, Microsoft Semantic Machines
Victoria Lin, Salesforce
Honglei Liu, Facebook Research
Jian-Guang Lou, Microsoft Research Asia
Yi Luan, Google Research
Siva Reddy, Stanford
Matthew Richardson, Microsoft Research
Jinfeng Rao, Facebook Conversational AI
Sameer Singh, UC Irvine
Shuyi Song, Zhejiang University
Yangqiu Song, HKUST
Xiang Ren, USC
Lingfei Wu, IBM Research
Ziyu Yao, The Ohio State University
Mo Yu, IBM Research
Zhou Yu, UC Davis
Hamed Zamani, University of Massachussets Amherst

Invited Speakers:

Joyce Chai, University of Michigan
H V Jagadish, University of Michigan
Monica S. Lam, Stanford University
Percy Liang, Stanford University
Luke Zettlemoyer, University of Washington & Facebook AI Research (FAIR)
Imed Zitouni, Google

Table of Contents

This page intentionally left blank.

Conference Program

Friday, July 10, 2020

08:15–08:30 ***Opening remarks***

08:30–09:30 ***Invited Talk: Joyce Chai***

09:30–10:30 ***Invited Talk: Percy Liang***

10:30–10:45 ***Break***

10:45–11:00 *Answering Complex Questions by Combining Information from Curated and Extracted Knowledge Bases*
Nikita Bhutani, Xinyi Zheng, Kun Qian, Yunyao Li and H. Jagadish

11:00–11:15 *Unnatural Language Processing: Bridging the Gap Between Synthetic and Natural Language Data (Cross-submission)*
Alana Marzoev, Samuel Madden, M. Frans Kaashoek, Michael Cafarella and Jacob Andreas

11:15–11:30 *Towards Reversal-Based Textual Data Augmentation for NLI Problems with Opposable Classes*
Alexey Tarasov

11:30–12:30 ***Invited Talk: H V Jagadish***

12:30–13:30 ***Break***

13:30–14:30 ***Invited Talk: Imed Zitouni***

14:30–14:45 *Examination and Extension of Strategies for Improving Personalized Language Modeling via Interpolation*
Liqun Shao, Sahitya Mantravadi, Tom Manzini, Alejandro Buendia, Manon Knoertzer, Soundar Srinivasan and Chris Quirk

14:45–15:00 *A Multi-Modal Agent that Learns Concepts and Conditionals from Natural Language and Demonstrations (Cross-submussion)*
Toby Jia-Jun Li, Marissa Radensky, Justin Jia, Kirielle Singarajah, Tom Mitchell and Brad Myers

15:00–15:15 *Efficient Deployment of Conversational Natural Language Interfaces over Databases*
Anthony Colas, Trung Bui, Franck Dernoncourt, Moumita Sinha and Doo Soon Kim

Friday, July 10, 2020 (continued)

15:15–15:30 *Neural Multi-task Text Normalization and Sanitization with Pointer-Generator*
Hoang Nguyen and Sandro Cavallari

15:30–15:45 ***Break***

15:45–16:45 ***Invited Talk: Monica Lam***

16:45–17:45 ***Invited Talk: Luke Zettlemoyer***

17:45–17:50 ***Closing remarks***

Answering Complex Questions by Combining Information from Curated and Extracted Knowledge Bases

Nikita Bhutani[1*] **Xinyi Zheng**[1*] **Kun Qian**[2] **Yunyao Li**[2] **H V Jagadish**[1]
[1]University of Michigan, Ann Arbor
[2]IBM Research, Almaden
nbhutani@umich.edu, zxycarol@umich.edu, qian.kun@ibm.com,
yunyaoli@us.ibm.com jag@umich.edu

Abstract

Knowledge-based question answering (KB-QA) has long focused on simple questions that can be answered from a single knowledge source, a manually curated or an automatically extracted KB. In this work, we look at answering complex questions which often require combining information from multiple sources. We present a novel KB-QA system, MULTIQUE, which can map a complex question to a complex query pattern using a sequence of simple queries each targeted at a specific KB. It finds simple queries using a neural-network based model capable of collective inference over textual relations in extracted KB and ontological relations in curated KB. Experiments show that our proposed system outperforms previous KB-QA systems on benchmark datasets, ComplexWebQuestions and WebQuestionsSP.

1 Introduction

Knowledge-based question answering (KB-QA) computes answers to natural language questions based on a knowledge base. Some systems use a *curated* KB (Bollacker et al., 2008), and others use an *extracted* KB (Fader et al., 2014). The choice of the KB depends on its coverage and knowledge representation: a curated KB uses ontological relations but has limited coverage, while an extracted KB offers broad coverage with textual relations. Commonly, a KB-QA system finds answers by mapping the question to a structured query over the KB. For instance, example question 1 in Fig. 1 can be answered with a query (*Rihanna*, *place_of_birth*, ?) over a curated KB or (*Rihanna*, *'was born in'*, ?) over an extracted KB.

Most existing systems focus on simple questions answerable with a single KB. Limited efforts have been spent to support complex questions that require inference over multiple relations and entities. For instance, to answer question 2 in Fig. 1, we need to infer relations corresponding to expressions *'author of'* and *'attend'*. In practice, a single KB alone may not provide both high coverage and ontological knowledge to answer such questions. A curated KB might provide information about educational institutions, while an extracted KB might contain information about authorship. Leveraging multiple KBs to answer complex questions is an attractive approach but is seldom studied. Existing methods assume a simple abstraction (Fader et al., 2014) over the KBs and have limited ability to aggregate facts across KBs.

simple
1. Where was Rihanna born?

nesting
2. What college did the author of 'The Hobbit' attend?

conjunction
3. Which Portuguese speaking countries import fish from Brazil?

Figure 1: Simple vs Complex questions.

We aim to integrate inference over curated and extracted KBs for answering complex questions. Combining information from multiple sources offers two benefits: evidence scattered across multiple KBs can be aggregated, and evidence from different KBs can be used to complement each other. For instance, inference over ontological relation *book_author* can benefit from textual relation *'is written by'*. On the other hand, evidence matching *'attend'* may exclusively be in the curated KB.

Example 1 What college did the author of 'The Hobbit' attend?
Simple Queries:
G_1: *The_Hobbit 'is wrtten by' ?a.*
G_2: *?b person.education ?c . ?c institution ?x.*
Join: $G = G_1 \text{ join}_{?a=?b} G_2$
Evaluate: ans = University of Oxford

In this work, we propose a novel KB-QA sys-

* NB and XZ contributed equally to this work.

Proceedings of the First Workshop on Natural Language Interfaces, pages 1–10
July 10, 2020. ©2020 Association for Computational Linguistics
https://doi.org/10.18653/v1/P17

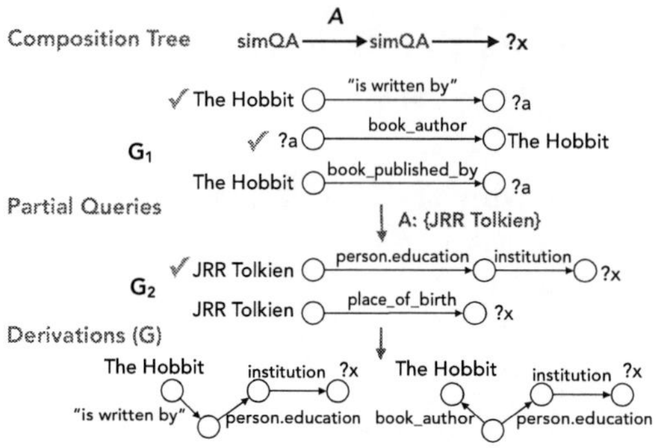

Figure 2: Partial queries and derivations.

tem, MULTIQUE, which constructs query patterns to answer complex questions from simple queries each targeting a specific KB. We build upon recent work on semantic parsing using neural network models (Bao et al., 2016; Yih et al., 2015) to learn the simple queries for complex questions. These methods follow an *enumerate-encode-compare* approach, where candidate queries are first collected and encoded as semantic vectors, which are then compared to the vector representation of the question. The candidate with the highest semantic similarity is then executed over the KB. We propose two key modifications to adapt these models to leverage information from multiple KBs and support complex questions. First, to enable collective inference over ontological and textual relations from the KBs, we align the different relation forms and learn unified semantic representations. Second, due to the lack of availability of fully-annotated queries to train the model, we learn with implicit supervision signals in the form of answers for questions. Our main contributions are:

- We propose a novel KB-QA system, MULTIQUE, that combines information from curated and extracted knowledge bases to answer complex questions. To the best of our knowledge, this is the first attempt to answer complex questions from multiple knowledge sources.
- To leverage information from multiple KBs, we construct query patterns for complex questions using simple queries each targeting a specific KB. (Section 3 and 5).
- We propose a neural-network based model that aligns diverse relation forms from multiple KBs for collective inference. The model learns to score simple queries using implicit supervision from answers to complex questions (Section 4).
- We provide extensive evaluation on benchmarks demonstrating the effectiveness of proposed

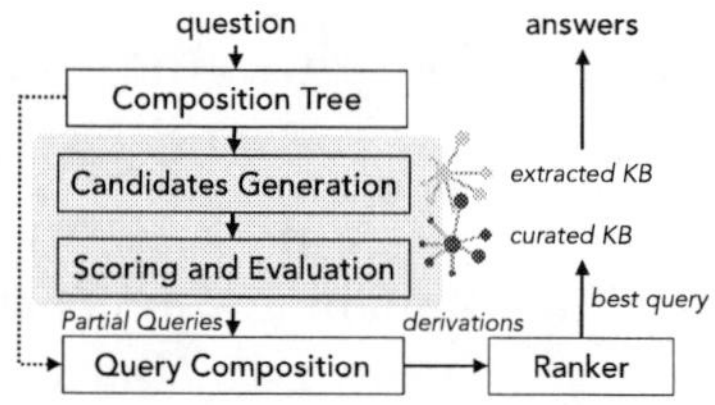

Figure 3: System Architecture

techniques on questions of varying complexity and KBs of different completeness (Section 6).

2 Task and Overview

Our goal is to map a complex question Q to a query G, which can be executed against a combination of curated KB $\mathcal{K}_c$ and extracted KB $\mathcal{K}_o$.

Knowledge Bases. The background knowledge source $\mathcal{K}=\bigcup\{\mathcal{K}_c, \mathcal{K}_o\}$ is denoted as $\mathcal{K}=(\mathcal{V}, \mathcal{E}, \mathcal{R})$, where $\mathcal{V}$ is the set of entities and $\mathcal{E}$ is a set of triples (s, r, o). A triple denotes a relation $r \in \mathcal{R}$ between subject $s \in \mathcal{V}$ and object $o \in \mathcal{V}$. The relation set $\mathcal{R}$ is a collection of ontological relations $\mathcal{R}^o$ from $\mathcal{K}_c$ and textual relations $\mathcal{R}^t$ from $\mathcal{K}_o$. A higher order relation is expressed using multiple triples connected using a special CVT node.

Complex Question, Q corresponds to a query G which has more than one relation and a single query focus $?x$. G is a sequence of partial queries $G = (G_1, G_2, .., G_o)$ connected via different join conditions. A partial query has four basic elements: a *seed* entity s^r is the root of the query, a *variable* node o^v corresponds to an answer to the query, a *main relation path* (s^r, p, o^v) is the path that links s^r to o^v by one or two edges from either R^o or R^t, and *constraints* take the form of an entity linked to the main relation by a relation c. By definition, each partial query targets a specific KB.

A composition tree C describes how the query G is constructed and evaluated given the partial queries. It includes two functions, *simQA* and *join*. *simQA* is the model for finding simple queries. It enumerates candidates for a simple query, encodes and compares them with the question representation, and evaluates the best candidate. *join* describes how to join two partial queries i.e. whether they share the query focus or another variable node. Fig. 2 shows the partial queries and composition tree for the running example 1.

Overview. Given a complex input question, the task is to first compute a composition tree that describes how to break down the inference into simple partial queries. We then have to gather can-

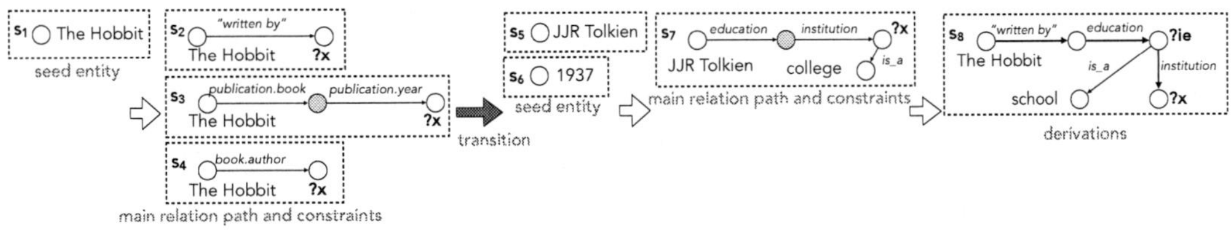

Figure 4: Example Candidate Generation for the running example 1.

didates for each partial query from both curated and extracted KBs. For each candidate, we have to measure its semantic similarity to the question using a neural-network based model that should be capable of inference over different forms of relations. We then have to join the different partial queries to find the complex query for the question. Since there can be multiple ways to answer a complex question, we derive several full query derivations. We rank them based on the semantic similarity scores of their partial queries, query structure and entity linking scores. We execute the *best* derivation over the multiple KBs. Fig. 3 shows the architecture of our proposed system, MULTIQUE.

3 Partial Query Candidate Generation

We first describe how we find candidates for partial queries given an input question. We use a staged generation method with *staged* states and actions. Compared to previous methods (Yih et al., 2015; Luo et al., 2018) which assume a question has one main relation, our strategy can handle complex questions which have multiple main relations (and hence partial queries). We include a new action A_t that denotes the end of the search for a partial query and transition to a state S_t. State S_t refers back to the composition tree to determine the join condition between the current partial query and the next query. If they share an answer node, candidate generation for the subsequent query can resume independently. Otherwise, it waits for the answers to the current query.

We generate (entity, mention) pairs for a question using entity linking (Bast and Haussmann, 2015) and then find elements for query candidates. Fig. 4 depicts our staged generation process.

Identify seed entity. The seed s^r for a partial query is a linked entity in the question or an answer of a previously evaluated partial query.

Identify main relation path. Given a seed entity, we consider all 1-hop and 2-hop paths p. These include both ontological and textual relations. The other end of the path is the variable node o^v.

Identify constraints. We next find entity and type constraints. We consider entities that can be connected using constraint relations *is_a* relations[1] to the variable node o^v. We also consider entities connected to the variables on the relation path via a single relation. We consider all subsets of constraints to enable queries with multiple constraints.

Transition to next partial query. Once candidates of a partial query G_i are collected, we refer to the composition tree to determine the start state of the next partial query G_{i+1}. If the next operation is *simQA*, we compute the semantic similarity of the candidates of G_i using our semantic matching model and evaluate K-best candidates. The answers form the seed for collecting candidates for G_{i+1}. Otherwise, candidate generation resumes with non-overlapping entity links in G_i.

4 Semantic Matching

We now describe our neural-network based model which infers over different relation forms and computes the semantic similarity of a partial query candidate to the question.

4.1 Model Architecture

Fig. 5 shows the architecture of our model. To encode the question, we replace all seed (constraint) entity mentions used in the query by dummy tokens w_E (w_C). To encode the partial query, we consider its query elements, namely the main relation path and constraint relations. Given the vector representations q for the question Q and g for the partial query G_i, we concatenate them and feed a multi-layer perceptron (MLP). The MLP outputs a scalar which we use as the semantic similarity $S_{sem}(Q, G_i)$. We describe in detail the encoding methods for the question and different relation forms in the main relation path. We also describe other design elements and the learning objective.

Encoding question. We encode a question Q using its token sequence and dependency structure.

[1] common.topic.notable_types,common.topic.notable_for

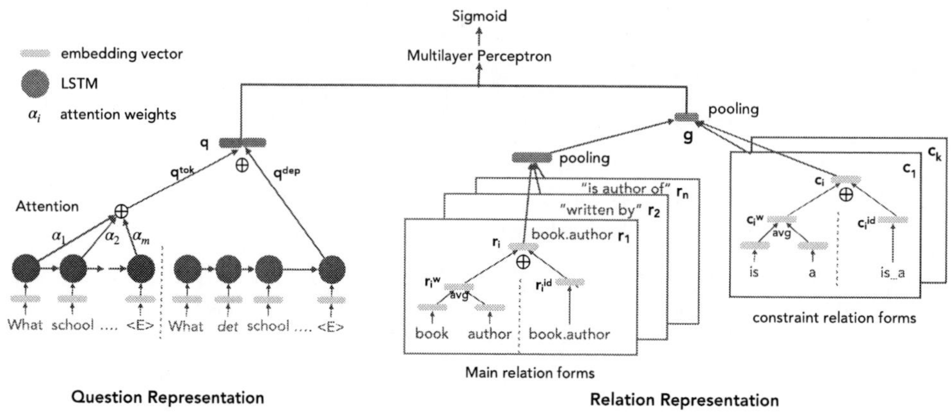

Figure 5: Semantic Matching Model

Since a complex question tends to be long, encoding its dependency tree captures any long-range dependencies. Let $\langle w_1, w_2, \ldots, w_n \rangle$ be the tokens in Q, where seed (constraint) entity mentions have been replaced with w_E (w_C). We map the tokens to vectors $\langle q_1^w, q_2^w, \ldots, q_n^w \rangle$ using an embedding matrix E_w and use an LSTM to encode the sequence to a latent vector q^w. Similarly, we encode the dependency tree into a latent vector q^{dep}.

Encoding main relation path. The main relation path can have different forms, a textual relation from $\mathcal{K}_o$ or an ontological relation from $\mathcal{K}_c$. In order to collectively infer over them in the same space, we first align the textual relations to ontological relations. For instance, we find textual relations *'is author of'*, *'written by'* can be aligned to ontological relation *book.author*. We describe how we derive the relation alignments in Sec. 4.2. Given a relation alignment, we encode each relation form i in the alignment to a latent vector r_i. We apply a max pooling over the latent vectors of different relations in the alignment to obtain a unified semantic representation over the different relation forms. Doing so enables the model to learn better representations of an ontological relation which has complementary textual relations.

To encode each relation form into vector r_i, we consider both sequence of tokens and ids (Luo et al., 2018). For instance, the id sequence of the relation in Fig. 5 is {*book_author*}, while its token sequence is {*'book'*, *'author'*}. We embed the tokens into vectors using an embedding matrix and use average embedding r^w as the token-level representation. We translate the relation directly using another embedding matrix E_r of relation paths to derive its id-level representation r_i^{id}. The vector representation of a path then is $r_i = [r_i^w; r_i^{id}]$.

Encoding constraints. Similarly, we encode the constraint relations c_i in by combining its token-level representation c_i^w and id-level representation c_i^{id}. Given the unified vector representation of a relation path, and the latent vectors of the constraint relations, we apply max pooling to obtain the compositional semantic representation g of the query.

Attention mechanism. Simple questions contain expressions for matching one main relation path. A complex question, however, has expressions for matching multiple relation paths, which could interfere with each other. For instance, words *'college'* and *'attend'* can distract the matching of the phrase *'author of'* to the relation *book.author*. We mitigate this issue by improving the question representation using an attention mechanism (Luong et al., 2015). The idea is to learn to emphasize parts of the question that are relevant to a context derived using the partial query vector g. Formally, given all hidden vectors h_t at time step $t \in \{1, 2, \ldots, n\}$ of the token-level representation of the question, we derive a context vector c as the weighted sum of all the hidden states:

$$c = \sum_{t=1}^{n} \alpha_t h_t$$

where α_t corresponds to an attention weight. The attention weights are computed as:

$$\alpha = softmax(W tanh(W_q q^w + W_g g))$$

where W, W_g, W_q are network parameters. The attention weights indicate how much the model focuses on each token given a partial query.

Objective function. We concatenate the context vector c, question dependency vector q^{dep} and query vector g and feed to a multi-layer perceptron (MLP). It is a feed-forward neural network with two hidden layers and a scalar output neuron indicating the semantic similarity score $S_{sem}(q, G_i)$. We train the model using cross entropy loss,

$$loss = ylog(S_{sem}) + (1-y)log(1-S_{sem})$$

where $y \in \{0, 1\}$ is a label indicating whether G_i is correct or not. Training the model requires a) an alignment of equivalent relation forms, and b) examples (question, partial query) pairs. We describe how we generate them given QA pairs.

4.2 Relation Alignment

An open KB has a huge vocabulary of relations. Aligning the textual relations to ontological relations for collective inference can become challenging if the textual relations are not canonicalized. We, first learn embeddings for the textual relations and cluster them to obtain canonicalized relation clusters (Vashishth et al., 2018). For instance, a cluster can include both *'is author of'* and *'authored'*. We use the canonicalized textual relations to derive an alignment to the ontological relations. We derive this alignment based on the support entity pairs (s, o) for a pair of ontological relation and canonicalized textual relation. For instance, relations *'is author of'* and *book.author* in our example question will share more entities than relations *'is author of'* and *education.institution*. The alignment is based on a support threshold i.e. minimum number of support entity pairs for a pair of relations. In our experiments, we set the threshold to 5 to avoid sparse and noisy signals in the alignment.

4.3 Implicit Supervision

Obtaining questions with fully-annotated queries is expensive, especially when queries are complex. In contrast, obtaining answers is easier. In such a setting, the quality of a query candidate is often measured indirectly by computing the F_1 score of its answers to the labeled answers (Peng et al., 2017a). However, for complex questions, answers to the partial queries may have little or no overlap with the labeled answers. We, therefore, adopt an alternative scoring strategy where we estimate the quality of a partial query as the best F_1 score of all its full query derivations. Formally, we compute a score $V(G_i^{(k)})$ for a partial query as:

$$V(G_i^{(k)}) = \max_{i \leq t \leq n-1} F_1(D_{t+1}^{(k)})$$

where D_t denotes the derivation at level t and n denotes the number of partial queries.

Such implicit supervision can be susceptible to spurious derivations which happen to evaluate to the correct answers but do not capture the semantic meaning of a question. We, thus, consider additional priors to promote true positive and false negative examples in the training data. We use $L(Q, G_i^{(k)})$ as the ratio of number of words in the relations of $G_i^{(k)}$ that are mentioned in the question Q. We also use $C(Q, G_i^{(k)})$ as the fraction of relation words that hit a small hand-crafted lexicon of co-occurring relation and question words. We estimate the quality of a candidate as: $V(G_i^{(k)}) + \gamma\, L(Q, G_i^{(k)}) + \delta\, C(Q, G_i^{(k)})$. We consider a candidate a positive example if its score is larger than a threshold (0.5) and negative otherwise.

5 Query Composition

In this work, we focus on constructing complex queries using a sequence of simple partial queries, each with one main relation path. Since the original question does not have to be chunked into simple questions, constructing composition trees for such questions is fairly simple. Heuristically, a composition tree can simply be derived by estimating the number of main relations (verb phrases) in the question and the dependency between them (subordinating or coordinating). We use a more sophisticated model (Talmor and Berant, 2018) to derive the composition tree. The post-order traversal of the tree yields the order in which partial queries should be executed.

Given a computation tree, we adopt a beam search and evaluate best k candidates for a partial query at each level. This helps maintain tractability in the large space of possible complex query derivations. The semantic matching model only independently scores the partial queries and not complete derivations. We, thus, need to find the best derivation that captures the meaning of the complex input question. To determine the best derivation, we aggregate the scores over the partial queries and consider additional features such as entities and structure of the query. We train a log-linear model on a set of (question-answer) pairs using features such as semantic similarity scores, entity linking scores, number of constraints in the query, number of variables, number of relations and number of answer entities. Given the best scoring derivation, we translate it to a KB query and evaluate it to return answers to the question. Such an approach has been shown to be successful in answering complex questions over a single knowledge base (Bhutani et al., 2019). In this work, we extend that approach to scenarios when multiple KBs are available.

6 Experiments

We present experiments that show MULTIQUE outperforms existing KB-QA systems on complex questions. Our approach to construct queries from simple queries and aggregate multiple KBs is superior to methods which map questions directly to queries and use raw text instead.

6.1 Experimental Setup

Datasets. We use two benchmark QA datasets:

- **CompQWeb** (Talmor and Berant, 2018): A recent dataset with highly complex questions with compositions, conjunctions, superlatives and comparatives. It contains 34,689 questions, split into 27,734 train, 3,480 dev and 3,475 test cases. For simplicity of evaluation, we only reserve questions with compositions and conjunctions (90% of the dataset).
- **WebQSP** (Yih et al., 2016): It contains 4,737 questions split into 3,098 train and 1,639 test cases. Most of the questions are simple; only 4% questions have multiple constraints (Yin et al., 2015). We evaluate on this dataset to demonstrate our proposed methods are effective on questions of varying complexity.

Knowledge Bases. We use the Freebase[2] dump as the curated KB. We construct an extracted KB using StanfordOpenIE (Angeli et al., 2015) over the snippets released by (Talmor and Berant, 2018) for CompQWeb and (Sun et al., 2018) for WebQSP.

Evaluation Metric. We report averaged F_1 scores of the predicted answers. We additionally compute precision@1 as the fraction of questions that were answered with the exact gold answer.

Baseline systems. We compare against two systems that can handle multiple knowledge sources.

- **GraftNet+** (Sun et al., 2018): Given a question, it identifies a KB subgraph potentially containing the answer, annotates it with text and performs a binary classification over the nodes in the subgraph to identify the answer node(s). We point that it collects subgraphs using 2-hop paths from a seed entity. Since this cannot scale for complex questions which can have arbitrary length paths, we follow our query composition strategy to generate subgraphs. We annotate the subgraphs with snippets released with the datasets. We call this approach GraftNet+.
- **OQA** (Fader et al., 2014): It is the first KB-QA system to combine curated KB and extracted KB. It uses a cascade of operators to paraphrase and parse questions to queries, and to rewrite and execute queries. It does not generate a unified representation of relation forms across the KBs. For comparison, we augment its knowledge source with our extracted KB and evaluate the model released by the authors.

Several other KB-QA systems (Cui et al., 2017; Abujabal et al., 2017; Bao et al., 2016) use only Freebase and handle simple questions with a few constraints. SplitQA (Talmor and Berant, 2018) and MHQA (Song et al., 2018) handle complex questions, but use web as the knowledge source.

Implementation Details. We used NVIDIA GeForce GTX 1080 Ti GPU for our experiments. We initialize word embeddings using GloVe (Pennington et al., 2014) word vectors of dimension 300. We use BiLSTMs to encode the question token and dependency sequences. We use 1024 as the size of hidden layer of MLP and *sigmoid* as the activation function.

6.2 Results and Discussion

We evaluate several configurations. We consider candidates from curated KB as the only available knowledge source to answer questions and use it as a baseline (*cKB-only*). To demonstrate that inference over curated KB can benefit from open KB, we consider diverse relation forms of curated KB facts from open KB (*cKB+oKB*). Lastly, we downsample the curated KB candidates to 90%, 75% and 50% to simulate incompleteness in KB.

Effectiveness on complex questions. Our proposed system outperforms existing approaches on answering complex questions (Table 1). Even though both MULTIQUE and GraftNet+ use the same information sources, our semantic matching model outperforms node classification. Also, using extracted facts instead of raw text enables us to exploit the relations between entities in the text. We also achieve significantly higher F_1 than OQA that uses multiple KB but relies on templates for parsing questions to queries directly and does not deeply integrate information from multiple KBs.

[2]http://commondatastorage.googleapis.com/freebase-public/rdf/freebase-rdf-2015-08-02-00-00.gz

Method	CompQWeb	WebQSP
MULTIQUE (cKB-only)	31.24/37.61	**61.16/69.84**
MULTIQUE (cKB+oKB)	**34.62/41.23**	57.49/67.51
MULTIQUE (90%cKB+oKB)	27.15/30.21	55.47/65.42
MULTIQUE (75%cKB+oKB)	25.54/28.09	50.64/60.17
MULTIQUE (50%cKB+oKB)	18.57/20.51	41.72/50.82
GraftNet+ (Sun et al., 2018)	31.96/44.78	57.21/68.98
OQA (Fader et al., 2014)	0.42/42.85	21.78/32.63
SplitQA(Talmor and Berant, 2018)	-/27.50	-
MHQA (Song et al., 2018)	-/30.10	-

Table 1: Average F_1 / precision@1 of baseline systems and MULTIQUE in different configurations.

In contrast, we can construct complex query patterns from simple queries, and can infer over diverse relation forms in the KB facts. SplitQA (Talmor and Berant, 2018) and MHQA (Song et al., 2018) use a similar approach to answer complex questions using a sequence of simpler questions, but rely solely on noisy web data. Clearly, by combining the knowledge from curated KB, we can answer complex questions more reliably.

Effectiveness on simple questions. An evaluation on simpler questions demonstrates that MULTIQUE can adapt to questions of varying complexity. We achieve the comparable F_1 score on the as other KB-QA systems that adopt an enumerate-encode-compare strategy. STAGG (Yih et al., 2015), a popular KB-QA system uses a similar approach for candidate generation but improves the results using feature engineering and by augmenting entity linking with external knowledge and only uses curated KB. MULTIQUE uses multiple KBs, and can be integrated with a better entity linking and scoring scheme for derivations.

KB completeness. Our results show that including information from extracted KB helps improve inference over ontological relations and facts for complex questions (as indicated by 3.38 F_1 gain in cKB+oKB). It instead hurts the performance on WebQSP dataset. This can be attributed to the coverage of the accompanying textual data sources of the two datasets. We found that for only 26% of the questions in WebQSP, an extracted fact could be aligned with a curated KB candidate. In contrast, there were 55% such questions in the CompQWeb. This illustrates that considering irrelevant, noisy facts does not benefit when curated KB is complete. Such issues can be mitigated by using a more robust retrieval mechanism for text snippets or facts from extracted KB.

A KB-QA system must rely on an extracted KB when curated KB is incomplete. This is reflected in the dramatic increase in the percentage of hybrid queries when curated KB candidates were downsampled (e.g., from 17% to 40% at 90% completeness). As expected, the overall F_1 drops because the precise curated KB facts become unavailable. Despite the noise in extracted KBs, we found 5-15% of the hybrid queries found a correct answer. Surprisingly, we find 55% of the queries changed when the KB is downsampled to 90%, but 89% of them did not hurt the average F_1. This indicates that the system could find alternative queries when KB candidates are dropped.

Setup	CompQWeb	WebQSP
No constraints	31.23/37.87	52.53/60.84
No attention	26.92/31.24	40.29/51.86
No re-ranking	29.39/36.14	55.13/62.78
No prior	30.88/36.68	57.54/64.63

Table 2: Ablation results, average F_1 / precision@1, of MULTIQUE (cKB+oKB).

Ablation Study. Queries for complex questions often have additional constraints on the main relation path. 35% of the queries in CompQWeb had at least one constraint, while most of the queries (85%) in WebQSP are simple. Ignoring constraints in candidate generation and in semantic matching drops the overall F_1 score by 9.8% (8.6%) on CompQWeb (WebQSP) (see Table 2). Complex questions also are long and contain expressions for matching different relation paths. Including the attention mechanism helps focus on relevant parts of the question and improves the relation inference. We found F_1 drops significantly on CompQWeb when attention is disabled.

Re-ranking complete query derivations by additionally considering entity linking scores and query structure consistently helps find better queries. We examined the quality of top-k query derivations (see Table 3). For a large majority of the questions, query with the highest F_1 score was among the top-10 candidates. A better re-ranking model, thus, could help achieve higher F_1 score. We also observed that incorporating prior domain knowledge in deriving labels for partial queries at training was useful for complex questions.

Qualitative Analysis. The datasets also provide queries over Freebase. We used them to analyze the quality of our training data and the queries generated by our system. We derive labels for each partial query candidate by comparing it to the labeled query. On an average, 4 candidates per ques-

	CompQWeb		WebQSP	
	%	Avg. *best* F_1	%	Avg. *best* F_1
Top-1	35.11	34.62	69.12	57.49
Top-2	39.73	37.02	76.21	63.74
Top-5	51.12	42.08	85.05	70.00
Top-10	59.19	46.39	89.63	73.37

Table 3: Percentage of questions with the highest F_1 score in the top-k derivations, and the average best F_1.

tion were labeled correct. We then compare them with the labels derived using implicit supervision. We found on average 3.06 partial queries were true positives and 103.08 were true negatives, with few false positives (1.72) and false negatives (0.78).

We further examined if the queries which achieve a non-zero F_1 were spurious. We compared the query components (entities, relations, filter clauses, ordering constraints) of such queries with labeled queries. We found high precision (81.89%) and recall (76.19%) of query components, indicating the queries were indeed precise.

Error Analysis. We randomly sampled 50 questions which achieve low F_1 score (< 0.1) and analyzed the queries manually. We found 38% errors were made because of incorrect entities in the query. 92% of the entity linking errors were made at the first partial query. These errors get propagated because we find candidate queries using a staged generation. A better entity linking system can help boost the overall performance. 12% of the queries had an incorrect curated KB relation and 18% of the queries had an incorrect extracted KB relation. In a large fraction of cases (32%) the predicted and true relation paths were ambiguous given the question (e.g., *kingdom.rulers* vs *government* for *"Which queen presides over the location..."*). This indicates that relation inference is difficult for highly similar relation forms.

Future Work. Future KB-QA systems targeting multiple KBs should address two key challenges. They should model whether a simple query is answerable from a given a KB or not. It should query the reliable, extracted KBs only when the curated KB lacks sufficient evidence. This could help improve overall precision. Second, while resolving multiple query components simultaneous is beneficial, the inference could be improved if the question representation reflected all prior inferences.

7 Related Work

KB-QA methods can be broadly classified into: retrieval-based methods, template-based methods and semantic parsing-based methods. Retrieval-based methods use relation extraction (Feng et al., 2016) or distributed representations (Bordes et al., 2014; Xu et al., 2016) to identify answers from the KB but cannot handle questions where multiple entities and relations have to be identified and aggregated. Template-based methods rely on manually-crafted templates which can encode very complex query logic (Unger et al., 2012; Zou et al., 2014), but suffer from the limited coverage of templates. Our approach is inspired by (Abujabal et al., 2017), which decomposes complex questions to simple questions answerable from simple templates. However, we learn solely from question-answer pairs and leverage multiple KBs.

Modern KB-QA systems use neural network models for semantic matching. These use an encode-compare approach (Luo et al., 2018; Yih et al., 2015; Yu et al., 2017), wherein continuous representations of question and query candidates are compared to pick a candidate which is executed to find answers. These methods require question-answer pairs as training data and focus on a single knowledge source. Combining multiple knowledge sources in KB-QA has been studied before, but predominantly for textual data. (Das et al., 2017b) uses memory networks and universal schema to support inference on the union of KB and text. (Sun et al., 2018) enriches KB subgraphs with entity links from text documents and formulates KB-QA as a node classification task. The key limitations for these methods are that a) they cannot handle highly compositional questions and b) they ignore the relational structure between the entities in the text. Our proposed system additionally uses an extracted KB that explicitly models the relations between entities and can compose complex queries from simple queries.

We formulate complex query construction as a search problem. This is broadly related to structured output prediction (Peng et al., 2017b) and path finding (Xiong et al., 2017; Das et al., 2017a) methods which learn to navigate the search space using supervision from question-answer pairs. These methods are effective for answering simple questions because the search space is small and the rewards to guide the search can be estimated reliably. We extend the ideas of learning from implicit supervision (Liang et al., 2016) and integrate it with partial query evaluation and priors to preserve the supervision signals.

8 Conclusion

We have presented a new KB-QA system that uses both curated and extracted KBs to answer complex questions. It composes complex queries using simpler queries each targeting a KB. It integrates an enumerate-encode-compare approach and a novel neural-network based semantic matching model to find partial queries. Our system outperforms existing state-of-the-art systems on highly compositional questions, while achieving comparable performance on simple questions.

References

Abdalghani Abujabal, Mohamed Yahya, Mirek Riedewald, and Gerhard Weikum. 2017. Automated template generation for question answering over knowledge graphs. In *Proc. WWW '17*, pages 1191–1200. International World Wide Web Conferences Steering Committee.

Gabor Angeli, Melvin Jose Johnson Premkumar, and Christopher D Manning. 2015. Leveraging linguistic structure for open domain information extraction. In *Proc. ACL '15*, volume 1, pages 344–354.

Junwei Bao, Nan Duan, Zhao Yan, Ming Zhou, and Tiejun Zhao. 2016. Constraint-based question answering with knowledge graph. In *Proc. COLING '16*, pages 2503–2514.

Hannah Bast and Elmar Haussmann. 2015. More accurate question answering on freebase. In *Proc. CIKM '15*, pages 1431–1440. ACM.

Nikita Bhutani, Xinyi Zheng, and HV Jagadish. 2019. Learning to answer complex questions over knowledge bases with query composition. In *Proceedings of the 28th ACM International Conference on Information and Knowledge Management*, pages 739–748.

Kurt D. Bollacker, Colin Evans, Praveen Paritosh, Tim Sturge, and Jamie Taylor. 2008. Freebase: a collaboratively created graph database for structuring human knowledge. In *Proc. SIGMOD '08*, pages 1247–1250. ACM.

Antoine Bordes, Jason Weston, and Nicolas Usunier. 2014. Open question answering with weakly supervised embedding models. In *Proc. ECML '14*, volume 8724, pages 165–180. Springer.

Wanyun Cui, Yanghua Xiao, Haixun Wang, Yangqiu Song, Seung-won Hwang, and Wei Wang. 2017. Kbqa: learning question answering over qa corpora and knowledge bases. *Proc. VLDB '17*, 10(5):565–576.

Rajarshi Das, Shehzaad Dhuliawala, Manzil Zaheer, Luke Vilnis, Ishan Durugkar, Akshay Krishnamurthy, Alex Smola, and Andrew McCallum. 2017a. Go for a walk and arrive at the answer: Reasoning over paths in knowledge bases using reinforcement learning. *arXiv preprint arXiv:1711.05851*.

Rajarshi Das, Manzil Zaheer, Siva Reddy, and Andrew McCallum. 2017b. Question answering on knowledge bases and text using universal schema and memory networks. In *Proc. ACL '17*, pages 358–365.

Anthony Fader, Luke Zettlemoyer, and Oren Etzioni. 2014. Open question answering over curated and extracted knowledge bases. In *Proc. SIGKDD ' 14*, pages 1156–1165. ACM.

Yansong Feng, Songfang Huang, Dongyan Zhao, et al. 2016. Hybrid question answering over knowledge base and free text. In *Proc. COLING '16*, pages 2397–2407.

Chen Liang, Jonathan Berant, Quoc Le, Kenneth D Forbus, and Ni Lao. 2016. Neural symbolic machines: Learning semantic parsers on freebase with weak supervision. *arXiv preprint arXiv:1611.00020*.

Kangqi Luo, Fengli Lin, Xusheng Luo, and Kenny Q. Zhu. 2018. Knowledge base question answering via encoding of complex query graphs. In *Proc. EMNLP '18*, pages 2185–2194.

Thang Luong, Hieu Pham, and Christopher D. Manning. 2015. Effective approaches to attention-based neural machine translation. In *Proc. EMNLP '15*, pages 1412–1421.

Haoruo Peng, Ming-Wei Chang, and Wen-tau Yih. 2017a. Maximum margin reward networks for learning from explicit and implicit supervision. In *Proc. EMNLP '17*, pages 2368–2378.

Haoruo Peng, Ming-Wei Chang, and Wen-tau Yih. 2017b. Maximum margin reward networks for learning from explicit and implicit supervision. In *Proc. EMNLP '17*, pages 2368–2378.

Jeffrey Pennington, Richard Socher, and Christopher Manning. 2014. Glove: Global vectors for word representation. In *Proc. EMNLP '14*, pages 1532–1543.

Linfeng Song, Zhiguo Wang, Mo Yu, Yue Zhang, Radu Florian, and Daniel Gildea. 2018. Exploring graph-structured passage representation for multi-hop reading comprehension with graph neural networks. *arXiv preprint arXiv:1809.02040*.

Haitian Sun, Bhuwan Dhingra, Manzil Zaheer, Kathryn Mazaitis, Ruslan Salakhutdinov, and William Cohen. 2018. Open domain question answering using early fusion of knowledge bases and text. In *Proc. EMNLP '18*, pages 4231–4242.

Alon Talmor and Jonathan Berant. 2018. The web as a knowledge-base for answering complex questions. In *Proc. NAACL '18*, pages 641–651.

Christina Unger, Lorenz Bühmann, Jens Lehmann, Axel-Cyrille Ngonga Ngomo, Daniel Gerber, and Philipp Cimiano. 2012. Template-based question answering over rdf data. In *Proc. WWW '12*, pages 639–648. ACM.

Shikhar Vashishth, Prince Jain, and Partha Talukdar. 2018. Cesi: Canonicalizing open knowledge bases using embeddings and side information. In *Proc. WWW '18*, pages 1317–1327. International World Wide Web Conferences Steering Committee.

Wenhan Xiong, Thien Hoang, and William Yang Wang. 2017. Deeppath: A reinforcement learning method for knowledge graph reasoning. In *Proc. EMNLP '17*, pages 564–573.

Kun Xu, Siva Reddy, Yansong Feng, Songfang Huang, and Dongyan Zhao. 2016. Question answering on freebase via relation extraction and textual evidence. In *Proc. ACL '16*.

Wen-tau Yih, Ming-Wei Chang, Xiaodong He, and Jianfeng Gao. 2015. Semantic parsing via staged query graph generation: Question answering with knowledge base. In *Proc. ACL '15*, pages 1321–1331.

Wen-tau Yih, Matthew Richardson, Chris Meek, Ming-Wei Chang, and Jina Suh. 2016. The value of semantic parse labeling for knowledge base question answering. In *Proc. ACL '16*, volume 2, pages 201–206.

Pengcheng Yin, Nan Duan, Ben Kao, Junwei Bao, and Ming Zhou. 2015. Answering questions with complex semantic constraints on open knowledge bases. In *Proceedings of the 24th ACM International on Conference on Information and Knowledge Management*, pages 1301–1310. ACM.

Mo Yu, Wenpeng Yin, Kazi Saidul Hasan, Cicero dos Santos, Bing Xiang, and Bowen Zhou. 2017. Improved neural relation detection for knowledge base question answering. *arXiv preprint arXiv:1704.06194*.

Lei Zou, Ruizhe Huang, Haixun Wang, Jeffrey Xu Yu, Wenqiang He, and Dongyan Zhao. 2014. Natural language question answering over rdf: a graph data driven approach. In *Proc. SIGMOD '14*, pages 313–324. ACM.

Towards Reversal-Based Textual Data Augmentation for NLI Problems with Opposable Classes

Alexey Tarasov
Informatica CLAIRE
1 Windmill Lane
Dublin 2, Ireland
atarasov@informatica.com

Abstract

Data augmentation methods are commonly used in computer vision and speech. However, in domains dealing with textual data, such techniques are not that common. Most of the existing methods rely on rephrasing, i.e. new sentences are generated by changing a source sentence, preserving its meaning. We argue that in tasks with opposable classes (such as "Positive" and "Negative" in sentiment analysis), it might be beneficial to also "invert" the source sentence, reversing its meaning, to generate examples of the opposing class. Methods that use somewhat similar intuition exist in the space of adversarial learning, but are not always applicable to text classification (in our experiments, some of them were even detrimental to the resulting classifier accuracy). We propose and evaluate two reversal-based methods on an NLI task of recognising a type of a simple logical expression from its description in plain-text form. After gathering a dataset on MTurk, we show that a simple heuristic using notion of negating the main verb has potential not only on its own, but that it can also boost existing state-of-the-art rephrasing-based approaches.

1 Introduction

In natural language processing (NLP), the high performance of a machine learning solution often depends on the quality and quantity of training data, but its collection is not always trivial (Wei and Zou, 2019). For some tasks, such as sentiment analysis, extensive corpora already exist, and can be used at least as a starting point. However, in the area of natural language interfaces (NLIs), tasks are often very specific, and training data often has to be collected from scratch, which can be a major limiting factor.

Data augmentation is a family of techniques that take an initial dataset (often limited in size) and automatically generate more examples, with the hope that they will introduce some realistic variability, thus reducing reliance on possibly costly and time-consuming data collection.

In some areas, good data augmentation approaches are available and widely used. For instance, to augment an image, one can scale it (Lecun et al., 1998) or crop it (Szegedy et al., 2015). Data augmentation is not limited just to computer graphics. For instance, Lee et al. (2005) proposed an augmentation approach for a more narrow area of schema matching. However, in NLP, usage of data augmentation is somewhat limited (Kobayashi, 2018). Currently, it is a very active area of research, and multiple different approaches are used. Almost all of them, however, rely on the same fundamental principle: to augment a sentence, generate sentences that have the same meaning, but use slightly different phrasing.

One of the limitations of such "rephrasing-based" approaches is that when applied to a sentence labelled with a certain class label, they can only generate sentences that belong to the same class. For instance, Wang and Yang (2015) proposed to replace certain words in a sentence with their synonyms. Applying such an approach to a positive review "This is a good movie" can result in "This is a fantastic movie", "This is a good film" and so on, but all of them will still be positive reviews. In this paper, we propose a different approach: instead of preserving the meaning of the sentence intact, we attempt to reverse its meaning, so that the "opposite" class can also benefit from data augmentation. To the best of our knowledge, limited attention has been paid to investigating such approaches, with the exception of few papers in the domain of adversarial learning (Jia and Liang 2017, Niu and Bansal 2018).

Reversing polarity of a free-text snippet, such as a movie review or a tweet, can be challenging and

Proceedings of the First Workshop on Natural Language Interfaces, pages 11–19

https://doi.org/10.18653/v1/P17

Pair	Classes	Sentence example	Expression example	Count
Particular value	=	X must be ten characters	$LENGTH(X) = 10$	93
	!=	X can not be 2	$X \neq 2$	126
Inequality	<	X shall not exceed 0	$X \leq 0$	239
	>	X is longer than 10	$LENGTH(X) > 10$	320
Null check	IS NULL	X is blank	$X\ IS\ NULL$	36
	NOT NULL	X cannot be missing	$X\ IS\ NOT\ NULL$	37
			Total	**851**

Table 1: Details of the dataset collected on MTurk for classifying the type of a logical expression, based on its textual description. Classes are divided into three pairs, and classes in the same pair are exact opposites of each other. I.e. negating a sentence belonging to one class should almost always result in a sentence belonging to the other class in the same pair.

even impossible, if done automatically. In this preliminary investigation we are limiting ourselves to short, relatively technical sentences, which are very common in NLI space. Using reversal of meaning for data augmentation can be useful for the tasks which have "naturally opposable" classes, for instance, in voice assistant dealing with opposite actions ("Set the alarm for 7am" vs. "Unset the alarm for 7am" or "Turn the volume down" vs. "Turn the volume up").

Our motivating example is understanding a logical statement, expressed as a short sentence in natural language. We were dealing with the first step of this task, recognising one of six statement types, which constitute three "naturally opposable" pairs. One of such pairs is "Equal"/"Not equal". By taking an example that belongs to "Equal" class such as "X is equal to two", we can reverse its meaning to "X is not equal to two", and in such way augment "Not equal" class as well. As far as we know, it is the first attempt to use such a technique for textual data augmentation in text classification tasks.

The main contributions of this paper are the following:

1. Dataset for a task of classifying type of logical statement, gathered on MTurk platform and consisting of 851 sentences, belonging to six classes.

2. Preliminary investigation of two approaches—*Main verb inversion* and *Adjective and adverb antonymy*—for performing textual data augmentation for tasks with "naturally opposable" classes. Our evaluation strongly suggests that *Main verb inversion* can increase the performance of a classifier and can also generate data, which cannot be acquired by using state-of-the-art rephrasing-based approaches.

The rest of the paper is structured as follows. In Section 2, we outline the task and describe data collection. Section 3 follows with an overview of related research. Section 4 describes our approaches in detail, and is followed by Section 5 outlining our evaluation methodology. Experimental results are discussed in Section 6, while Section 7 concludes the paper and proposes directions for future work.

2 Task and data collection

The motivational application behind our experiments is the task of translating a sentence in natural language into a logical expression that otherwise would have to be specified using complex and not very user-friendly language, such as SQL (or a formula editor in a tool such as Excel). This task can be solved in different ways, and some of them rely on inferring statement type (or its intent) as the first step.

We were concerned with six such types that were divided into three pairs, where classes in each pair are exact opposites. It means that if the meaning of a sentence from one pair class is reversed, we get a sentence that belongs to the second class in the same pair. An overview of all classes with examples is given in Table 1. We were interested in 31 logical expressions, some examples of which are listed in *Expression example* column.

A variety of free-text phrases can be used to describe the same logical expression. For instance, "$X\ IS\ NULL$" can be phrased as "X is blank", "X should not be empty", "X should be populated in all cases" and so on. We wanted to get a reliable expression type detector that would be robust to such examples of language variability.

We collected the data on Amazon Mechanical Turk platform. A single HIT presented a logical statement (such as "$LENGTH(X) > 0$" or "$X < 0$"), and a turker had to provide four significantly different phrases, that describe the logic in natural language.

First, we performed a quick pilot collection to make sure that our instructions and setup make sense, involving only Master turkers. No problems were encountered, so we proceeded with the main data collection, involving only turkers with acceptance rate on previous tasks of at least 60%. Each HIT was completed by at least 10 workers, and we paid $0.20 for every successful completion[1].

We had to reject about 35% of submitted HITs due to imprecise or spammy answers. Additionally, some of the accepted answers were same, for instance, expression "$X\ IS\ NULL$" was often transcribed as "X must be empty". After eliminating such duplicates, we got a dataset of 851 sentences, achieving good balance inside each pair of classes. The resulting dataset is publicly available online[2].

Next section describes existing data augmentation methods. We discuss methods that try to preserve the meaning of the original sentence (majority of them), as well as few exceptions.

3 Related research

Textual data augmentation was used in a number of different areas, including text classification (Wei and Zou, 2019), textual (Yu et al., 2018) or visual question answering (Kafle et al., 2017), reading comprehension systems (Jia and Liang, 2017) and machine translation (Fadaee et al., 2017, Gao et al., 2019). In fields like computer vision or speech, there are well-established methods that work across many applications, such as introducing random noise into an audio clip or cropping an image. However, according to Kobayashi (2018), in the field of NLP, it is very difficult to come up with an approach that would be easily applicable to various tasks. It can explain existence of a variety of augmentation strategies, most of which can be broadly categorised into two big categories: strategies that rephrase a sentence preserving its original meaning, and strategies that deliberately change the meaning of a sentence.

[1]Median completion time for a HIT was 204 seconds.

[2]`https://github.com/alexey-tarasov-irl/acl2020_nli_workshop`

3.1 "Preserve the meaning" augmentation

All these approaches attempt rephrasing a sentence, while keeping its original semantics. It can be done in a variety of ways:

1. **Generative approaches** employ a deep generative model (Bowman et al., 2016, Hu et al., 2017) to generate sentences with desired attributes from a continuous space. According to Wu et al. (2019), they often generate sentences that aren't readable and do not correspond to the desired class labels.

2. **Random permutation**: new sentences are generated by applying a very simple randomised heuristic to a source sentence, such as deleting (Iyyer et al., 2015, Wei and Zou, 2019, Xie et al., 2017) or swapping words (Artetxe et al., 2018, Niu and Bansal, 2018).

3. **Backtranslation**: a source sentence is translated into a different language (pivotal language), and then the result is translated back into the language of the source sentence (Sennrich et al., 2016, Yu et al., 2018). For example, using German as pivotal language can result in a sequence like "X is lower than 0" →"X ist kleiner als 0" →"X is less than 0".

4. **Synonym usage**: very commonly used strategies which usually involve selecting a word in a source sentence and then replacing it with a synonym. Sometimes words to be replaced are chosen randomly (Wei and Zou, 2019), while other researchers impose some limitations, such as only changing the headword (Kolomiyets et al., 2011). Ways to find synonyms range from relatively low-tech, such as using WordNet synsets (Wei and Zou, 2019, Zhang et al., 2015), to much more advanced approaches involving word embeddings (Wang and Yang, 2015) or bi-directional deep learning models (Kobayashi, 2018, Wu et al., 2019).

All these strategies have their own advantages and drawbacks, so many text augmentation approaches use a hybrid strategy, such as Easy Data Augmentation (EDA) by Wei and Zou (2019). It uses a combination of random permutation strategies and synonyms. One of its parameters n_{aug} is the maximum number of new sentences to generate per each source sentence. It is a recent and simple algorithm that embodies a lot of very commonly used text augmentation techniques. The results of Wei and Zou (2019) indicate that it achieves performance similar to much more complex algorithms, but is much quicker and doesn't rely on external dataset or language models.

3.2 "Change the meaning" augmentation

In some applications, it might be beneficial to deliberately change the meaning of a sentence, instead of preserving it. It is often done in the domain of *adversarial learning* for two purposes:

- **Purpose #1:** investigate whether a model can be confused by deliberately misleading data.
- **Purpose #2:** make the model robust against such adversarial attacks.

Niu and Bansal (2018) used dialogue models to predict the next turn, based on current context. They used reversal of meaning as a way to strengthen the model, making it more robust to changes in phrases that are very subtle yet change the meaning completely. They investigated two strategies[3]:

1. **Add negation**: for the first verb[4] in the sentence (going left to right), that doesn't have an outgoing `neg` arc in the dependency graph, the negation is artificially added. If no negation is detected, the original sentence is returned as augmented sentence (i.e. the approach always returns one sentence per each source sentence, effectively doubling the size of the original set).

2. **Antonym**: all words in the original sentence are picked one by one, going left to right[5]. For each such word, all synsets that have it are extracted, and all words in those synsets are explored for antonyms. The original word in the sentence is replaced by a random antonym from that set, and the process is over once one word in the original sentence is successfully replaced[6]. Thus, this strategy can increase the size of the dataset by 100% at the most.

Both approaches have been tested in four different conditions, varying datasets used for training and testing:

1. **Original train, original test**: the performance of the system on original test data, when no augmentation was performed.

2. **Original train, augmented test**: investigation into whether the system is robust enough to handle adversarial inputs (purpose #1 mentioned above).

3. **Augmented train, augmented test**: experiment to prove that augmenting training data with adversarial sentences makes the system more robust (purpose #2 above).

4. **Augmented train, original test**: checking whether augmenting training data helps with the model doing better on "usual", non-adversarial data.

In our setup, we were looking into augmenting training data, in order to make the classifier perform better on original data (Condition #4). However, Niu and Bansal (2018) failed to achieve statistically significant increase in #4, which suggests that both *Add negation* and *Antonym* might not be beneficial for our task.

Another augmentation approach that deliberately changes the meaning was proposed and evaluated by Jia and Liang (2017), for question answering systems. Their goal was not to make them more robust, but to show how easy it can be to confuse them. For each question in a corpus, they attempted to generate an adversarial sentence by replacing nouns and adjectives with antonyms from WordNet (very similar to *Antonym* by Niu and Bansal 2018), and change named entities and numbers to the nearest word in GloVe word vector space. For instance, "What ABC division handles domestic television distribution?" would become "What NBC [ABC replaced by a nearby word NBC] division handles

[3]The original paper offers a limited description of the approaches, so we relied on the accompanying source code located at `https://github.com/WolfNiu/AdversarialDialogue`.

[4]TreeBank POS. tags `VB`, `VBD`, `VBG`, `VBN`, `VBP`, `VBZ`.

[5]The paper states that it happens only for verbs, nouns, adjectives and adverbs, but the accompanying code actually just goes through all words, using part-of-speech only while searching for suitable synsets.

[6]In the original paper, each selected antonym had to also be present somewhere in the training corpus, usually, in a different sentence. It might be feasible if a large dataset is available, but in our case it would have resulted in almost no new sentences introduced. This is why we relaxed this condition in our experiments, and let *Antonyms* use antonyms, even if they are not present in any sentence in the dataset.

foreign [WordNet antonym to 'domestic'] television distribution?" Then, they generated a fake answer, which couldn't possibly be the right answer for this adversarial question. The experiments in the paper show that question answering systems can be easily fooled and often would produce that fake answer.

Work by Kaushik et al. (2020) serves as good evidence that inverting sentence meaning can be beneficial for text classification, both in terms of overall accuracy and robustness to adversarial data. However, instead of using automated rules, they asked crowdsourced workers to revert the meaning of a movie review, so that the document still remains coherent and a minimum of modifications is made.

To the best of our knowledge, automated methods from this subsection have never been applied to text classification tasks. Next section covers two approaches we propose in this paper.

4 Our approaches

Approach by Jia and Liang (2017), described in the previous section, is not directly applicable to our task, as replacing nouns and numbers won't result in effective negation of sentences in our dataset. The only useful aspect—antonyms of adjectives—is also present in paper by Niu and Bansal (2018), which also contains other useful insights.

We propose two approaches, that enhance *Add negation* and *Antonym* by Niu and Bansal (2018) described in Section 3.2:

1. Main verb inversion (enhancement of *Add negation*): similarly to *Add negation*, we add negation if it's not there, but in addition we also remove it if it is present.

2. Adjective and adverb antonymy (enhancement of *Antonym*): in our experience, *Antonym* often produced sentences that did not make grammatical sense, sentences with grammatical mistakes or sentences that were not proper negations of the original sentence. Table 2 provides a few examples of such issues. The most common root causes of such issues are the following:

1. Some antonyms selected from WordNet belonged to the wrong synset of the verb that was picked for replacement. For instance, the verb "can" is not only a modal verb, but is also an informal US expression for removing someone from their job. This is why for "can", in sentences like "X can be negative", *Antonym* picked the synset with the words "fire" and "give notice". The synset has "hire" as antonym, and that is the word that made its way into the augmented sentence ("X hire be positive"), which didn't make sense. Similar behaviour was observed for other common words such as "will".

2. When the adjective is replaced, its comparative/superlative form is not preserved (e.g. if "lower" is selected for replacement, it's replaced with "high", not "higher").

3. Due to its left-to-right nature, *Antonym* often picks an improper word for replacement. For instance, in sentence "X is no bigger than 2", it can't find any antonyms for "X" and "is", but picks "yes" as an antonym to "no", which results in "X is yes bigger than 2".

It might seem that both *Add negation* and *Antonym* by Niu and Bansal (2018) can result in a dataset of much lower quality, compared to the original. However, their intention was to pollute a sentence enough to change its meaning in some way, or make it incomprehensible, to deliberately confuse dialogue systems. However, we are trying to achieve something much more complicated. In our task, it's not enough to break the meaning of a sentence. We aim for coming up with valid sentences that properly negate the source sentence.

This is why our main assumption is that not producing a sentence at all is better than producing a sentence that doesn't make sense. We only replace adverbs and adjectives, and only if it's the only adverb/adjective in the sentence, and it is directly connected to the root. For each such sentence, we produce a new sentence for each antonym found in WordNet, and preserve comparative/superlative adjective forms.

5 Experiment methodology

The goal of our experiments was to investigate whether reversal-based data augmentation can boost accuracy in text classification tasks. We were concerned with two questions:

1. Is there a benefit in using reversal-based approaches, compared to not using data augmentation at all (Experiment #1)?

2. Can reversal-based approaches be a useful addition to already existing rephrasing-based augmentation techniques (Experiment #2)?

Source sentence	A correct augmentation	Augmentation by *Antonyms* (Niu and Bansal, 2018)
X can be negative	X can be positive	X **hire** be positive
X must be lower than 0	X must be higher than 0	X must be **high** than 0
X is no bigger than 2	X is no smaller than 2	X is **yes** bigger than 2

Table 2: Examples where *Antonym* approach (Niu and Bansal, 2018) provided highly incorrect sentences (bold text highlights mistakes that were made). See Section 4 for a detailed discussion.

5.1 Experiment #1: reversal-based augmentation vs. no augmentation

We used a CNN[7] proposed by Kim (2014), which is commonly used for evaluating data augmentation approaches (Park and Ahn 2019, Wei and Zou 2019). We ran it separately for each augmentation approach, conducting 5-fold cross validation augmenting only training data, leaving test partition intact. We allowed the training algorithm to run for 50 epochs of batch gradient descent (batch size = 64). A single sentence encoded using 50-dimensional GloVe embeddings (Pennington et al., 2014) was the input to the CNN (*Sentence example* column from Table 1).

We benchmarked both of our reversal-based augmentation approaches, proposed in Section 4, against the following baselines:

1. No augmentation
2. Add negation (Niu and Bansal, 2018)
3. Antonym (Niu and Bansal, 2018)

Our dataset was well-balanced by design; however, in many real-life applications it might not be the case. Potentially, augmentation approaches can be especially beneficial if applied to underrepresented classes. To simulate such a condition, in each training split, before performing augmentation, we artificially removed a fraction of instances belonging to classes ">", "!=" and "IS NULL" (leaving 25%, 50%, 75% intact) and only then performed data augmentation. We also tested the condition when no such undersampling was performed, and 100% of instances of those classes were retained.

Each experiment was conducted twenty-five times to counteract multiple random factors present in this setup, with average macro F1 reported as performance metric. Wilcoxon test was used to determine statistical significance of differences in performance.

5.2 Experiment #2: reversal-based on top of rephrasing-based

Even if reversal-based augmentation approaches are useful on their own, it is possible that they can't bring additional benefit if a rephrasing-based approach has already been used. To investigate this, overall, we followed the same methodology as in Experiment #1. Here is how we derived training data for each experimental condition.

In each cross-fold validation split, we applied EDA to training data[8], with default values of all parameters (including $n_{aug} = 9$). Then we applied an augmentation approach to the same training data, and merged its results with those coming from EDA. As before, test splits were not augmented, and we reported macro F1 score, averaged across twenty five experiments.

If reversal-based augmentation approaches work, CNN performance on such sets is expected to be higher than on just EDA on its own. However, performing EDA with $n_{aug} = 9$ and using it as a baseline would not have been fair: EDA in conjunction with any other augmentation approach is expected to result in a bigger dataset than EDA on its own. To make sure that any possible differences in accuracies cannot be attributed to this, we experimentally found a value of $n_{aug} = 11$, which guaranteed that the EDA baseline had a dataset, which is larger than any other set, resulting from applying augmentation.

6 Results

Results of Experiment #1 are given in Table 3. Both approaches by Niu and Bansal (2018) exposed very unreliable performance. In total, eight experiments involved them (four undersampling scenarios mul-

[7]Parameters (tuned on the full dataset): three convolution layers with window sizes of three, four and five (128 filters each); dropout rate of 0.25; Adam optimizer ($\eta = 0.001$, $\beta_1 = 0.9$, $\beta_2 = 0.999$).

[8]Using code from `https://github.com/jasonwei20/eda_nlp`

Augmentation approach	Dataset size	Relative change	Artificial undersampling, F1 25%	50%	75%	100%
No augmentation (baseline)	851	—	27.78	47.79	53.69	56.05
Antonym (Niu and Bansal, 2018)	1,591	+87%	**42.24▲**	49.25	51.41▼	54.16▼
Adjective and adverb antonymy (ours)	1,173	+38%	32.20▲	46.90	53.33	54.82
Add negation (Niu and Bansal, 2018)	1,702	+100%	45.20▲	50.29▲	52.87	53.18▼
Main verb inversion (ours)	1,517	+78%	**55.32▲**	**61.59▲**	**62.52▲**	**63.57▲**

Table 3: Results of Experiment #1: no augmentation baseline is compared to four reversal-based augmentation approaches. If an approach was significantly better than the baseline and another approach in the pair, its F1 is given in bold. ▼/▲ denote when approach was significantly worse/better than the baseline (Wilcoxon text, $p < 0.01$). *Relative change* indicates how big was the resulting dataset after augmentation (e.g. +100% means that it was twice the size of the original set).

Augmentation approach	Dataset size	Relative change	Artificial undersampling, F1 25%	50%	75%	100%
EDA (Wei and Zou, 2019), $n_{aug} = 11$	10,212	+1,100%	51.72	64.20	68.42	70.02
EDA (Wei and Zou, 2019), $n_{aug} = 9$						
+ Add negation (Niu and Bansal, 2018)	9,361	+1,000%	53.45	63.75	68.51	69.82
+ Main verb inversion (ours)	9,176	+978%	**57.65▲**	**67.36▲**	**70.46▲**	**72.06▲**

Table 4: Results of Experiment #2: EDA baseline is compared to EDA in conjunction with two verb-negation-oriented approaches. If an approach was significantly better than the others, its F1 is given in bold. ▲ denotes approaches that were significantly better than EDA baseline (Wilcoxon test, $p < 0.01$). *Relative change* indicates how big was the resulting dataset after augmentation.

tiplied by two approaches). In three out of eight, they worsened the performance of the classifier, in another two they didn't make any difference, and only in remaining three they made it significantly better. In contrast, both *Main verb inversion* and *Adjective and adverb antonymy* improved the performance significantly in more than half of the experiments, compared to no augmentation baseline. Additionally, *Main verb inversion* consistently showed results that were significantly better than both the baseline and *Add negation*. Usage of *Adjective and adverb antonymy* never harmed the performance, but it also rarely improved it. This is why we dropped both *Antonym* and *Adjective and adverb antonymy* from Experiment #2.

In Experiment #2 (Table 4), *Add negation* (Niu and Bansal, 2018) failed to improve the results of plain EDA significantly. At the same time, our *Main verb inversion* was significantly better than EDA in all experiments, which strongly suggests that it can derive data, not easily accessible by a rephrasing-based approach, such as EDA.

Overall, the results allow us to recommend *Main verb inversion* as a promising direction for textual data augmentation in classification tasks. Compared to no augmentation baseline, it improved macro F1 by 7.53–27.54pp (or by 13.42–99.15%), depending on how balanced the dataset is. *Main verb inversion* was especially beneficial when used to imbalanced datasets. When used on top of EDA, *Main verb inversion* was able to improve the F1 score by 2.04–5.93pp (or 2.92–11.47%).

7 Conclusions and future work

In this paper we addressed a problem of detecting a type of a logical statement from its textual description. We gathered our own task-specific dataset on MTurk, and then tried to boost the accuracy of the resulting classifier by applying textual data augmentation. We used two approaches (*Add negation* and *Antonym*) by Niu and Bansal (2018) from the current research in adversarial learning. In our experiments, neither of them could show stable improvement over a no-augmentation baseline. Even worse, often they had a detrimental effect on the macro F1 score of the resulting classifier.

We proposed two approaches: *Adjective and adverb antonymy* and *Main verb inversion*. The former failed to expose any benefit in our experiments; however, the latter consistently performed better than baselines. Despite its simplicity, it could achieve significantly better results than the no-augmentation baseline (improvement was ranging from 13% to 99%). *Main verb inversion* also showed the capability to introduce information into the training set, which is not available to state-of-the-art rephrasing-based approaches. A combination of EDA and *Main verb inversion* was 3–11% better than EDA on its own.

Main verb inversion showed promising performance, but it might be difficult to use it to negate sentences, expressed in less technical language (such as tweets or movie reviews). This is why enhancing its capabilities to other application areas seems to us like the primary direction for future work. It's unlikely that it can become a widely used cross-application approach in its current shape, but we hope that our findings will be thought-provoking for researchers who want to pursue reversal-based augmentation further. One of the possible improvements is to rely on a black-box model instead of heuristic rules (e.g. a sequence-to-sequence model that takes a sentence and returns the corresponding inverted sentence).

While verb negation/inversion showed good performance, approaches based on directly seeking antonyms proved to be ineffective. It might be interesting to investigate the reasons of their failure in more detail.

Acknowledgements

The author would like to thank Informatica CLAIRE team, especially, Bojan Furlan, Igor Balabine, AnHai Doan and Darshan Joshi for discussions, support and encouragement. Special thanks go to Awez Syed who sparkled author's interest in data augmentation. We would also like to express the deepest appreciation to Ashlee Bailey Brinan for her editorial comments that greatly improved the paper.

We thank three anonymous reviewers for their comments, and workers on MTurk for completing our tasks and making this work possible.

References

Mikel Artetxe, Gorka Labaka, Eneko Agirre, and Kyunghyun Cho. 2018. Unsupervised neural machine translation. In *Procs of ICLR*.

Samuel R. Bowman, Luke Vilnis, Oriol Vinyals, Andrew M. Dai, Rafal Jozefowicz, and Samy Bengio. 2016. Generating sentences from a continuous space. In *Procs of CoNLL*, pages 10–21.

Marzieh Fadaee, Arianna Bisazza, and Christof Monz. 2017. Data augmentation for low-Resource neural machine translation. In *Procs of ACL*, pages 567–573.

Fei Gao, Jinhua Zhu, Lijun Wu, Yingce Xia, Tao Qin, Xueqi Cheng, Wengang Zhou, and Tie-Yan Liu. 2019. Soft Contextual Data Augmentation for Neural Machine Translation. In *Procs of ACL*, pages 5539–5544.

Zhiting Hu, Zichao Yang, Xiaodan Liang, Ruslan Salakhutdinov, and Eric P. Xing. 2017. Toward controlled generation of text. In *ICML*, volume 4, pages 2503–2513.

Mohit Iyyer, Varun Manjunatha, Jordan Boyd-Graber, and Hal Daume III. 2015. Deep Unordered Composition Rivals Syntactic Methods for Text Classification. In *Procs of ACL*, pages 1681–1691.

Robin Jia and Percy Liang. 2017. Adversarial examples for evaluating reading comprehension systems. In *EMNLP 2017 - Conference on Empirical Methods in Natural Language Processing, Proceedings*, pages 2021–2031.

Kushal Kafle, Mohammed Yousefhussien, and Christopher Kanan. 2017. Data Augmentation for Visual Question Answering. In *Procs of Natural Language Generation conference*, pages 198–202.

Divyansh Kaushik, Eduard Hovy, and Zachary C. Lipton. 2020. Learning the Difference that Makes a Difference with Counterfactually-Augmented Data. In *Procs of ICLR*.

Yoon Kim. 2014. Convolutional neural networks for sentence classification. In *Procs of EMNLP*, pages 1746–1751.

Sosuke Kobayashi. 2018. Contextual Augmentation: Data Augmentation by Words with Paradigmatic Relations. In *Procs of NAACL*, pages 452–457.

Oleksandr Kolomiyets, Steven Bethard, and Marie Francine Moens. 2011. Model-portability experiments for textual temporal analysis. In *Procs of ACL-HLT*, volume 2, pages 271–276.

Yann Lecun, Leon Bottou, Yoshua Bengio, Patrick Ha, and Patrick Haffner. 1998. Gradient-Based Learning Applied to Document Recognition. *Proceedings of the IEEE*, 86(11).

Yoonkyong Lee, Mayssam Sayyadian, Anhai Doan, and Arnon S. Rosenthal. 2005. ETuner: Tuning schema matching software using synthetic scenarios. In *Procs of VLDB*.

Tong Niu and Mohit Bansal. 2018. Adversarial oversensitivity and over-stability strategies for dialogue models. In *Procs of CoNLL*, CoNLL, pages 486–496.

Dongju Park and Chang Wook Ahn. 2019. Self-supervised contextual data augmentation for natural language processing. *Symmetry*, 11(11).

Jeffrey Pennington, Richard Socher, and Christopher D. Manning. 2014. GloVe: Global Vectors for Word Representation. In *Procs of EMNLP*, pages 1532—-1543.

Rico Sennrich, Barry Haddow, and Alexandra Birch. 2016. Improving neural machine translation models with monolingual data. In *Procs of ACL*, pages 86–96.

Christian Szegedy, Wei Liu, Yangqing Jia, Pierre Sermanet, Scott Reed, Dragomir Anguelov, Dumitru Erhan, Vincent Vanhoucke, and Andrew Rabinovich. 2015. Going deeper with convolutions. In *Procs of IEEE CVPR*.

William Yang Wang and Diyi Yang. 2015. That's so annoying!!!: A lexical and frame-semantic embedding based data augmentation approach to automatic categorization of annoying behaviors using #petpeeve tweets. In *Procs of EMNLP*, pages 2557–2563.

Jason Wei and Kai Zou. 2019. EDA: Easy Data Augmentation Techniques for Boosting Performance on Text Classification Tasks. In *Procs of EMNLP*, pages 6382–6388.

Xing Wu, Shangwen Lv, Liangjun Zang, Jizhong Han, and Songlin Hu. 2019. Conditional BERT Contextual Augmentation. *Lecture Notes in Computer Science*, 11539 LNCS:84–95.

Ziang Xie, Sida I. Wang, Jiwei Li, Daniel Lévy, Aiming Nie, Dan Jurafsky, and Andrew Y. Ng. 2017. Data noising as smoothing in neural network language models. In *Procs of ICLR*.

Adams Wei Yu, David Dohan, Minh Thang Luong, Rui Zhao, Kai Chen, Mohammad Norouzi, and Quoc V. Le. 2018. QaNet: Combining local convolution with global self-attention for reading comprehension. In *Procs of ICLR*.

Xiang Zhang, Junbo Zhao, and Yann LeCun. 2015. Character-level Convolutional Networks for Text Classification. In *Procs of NIPS*, pages 649–657.

Examination and Extension of Strategies for Improving Personalized Language Modeling via Interpolation

Liqun Shao*, **Sahitya Mantravadi***, **Tom Manzini***, **Alejandro Buendia***, **Manon Knoertzer***, **Soundar Srinivasan, and Chris Quirk**
Microsoft Corp.
{*lishao,samantr,thmanzin,albuendi,maknoert,sosrini,chrisq*}@*microsoft.com*

Abstract

In this paper, we detail novel strategies for interpolating personalized language models and methods to handle out-of-vocabulary (OOV) tokens to improve personalized language models. Using publicly available data from Reddit, we demonstrate improvements in offline metrics at the user level by interpolating a global LSTM-based authoring model with a user-personalized n-gram model. By optimizing this approach with a back-off to uniform OOV penalty and the interpolation coefficient, we observe that over 80% of users receive a lift in perplexity, with an average of 5.2% in perplexity lift per user. In doing this research we extend previous work in building NLIs and improve the robustness of metrics for downstream tasks.

1 Introduction

Natural language interfaces (NLIs) have become a ubiquitous part of modern life. Such interfaces are used to converse with personal assistants (e.g., Apple Siri, Amazon Alexa, Google Assistant, Microsoft Cortana), to search for and gather information (Google, Bing), and to interact with others on social media. One developing use case is to aid the user during composition by suggesting words, phrases, sentences, and even paragraphs that complete the user's thoughts (Radford et al., 2019).

Personalization of these interfaces is a natural step forward in a world where the vocabulary, grammar, and language can differ hugely user to user (Ishikawa, 2015; Rabinovich et al., 2018). Numerous works have described personalization in NLIs in audio rendering devices (Morse, 2008), digital assistants (Chen et al., 2014), telephone interfaces (Partovi et al., 2005), etc. We explore an approach for personalization of language models (LMs) for use in downstream NLIs on composition assistance, and replicate previous work to show that interpolating a global long short-term memory network (LSTM) model with user-personalized n-gram models provides per-user performance improvements when compared with only a global LSTM model (Chen et al., 2015, 2019). We extend that work by providing new strategies to interpolate the predictions of these two models. We evaluate these strategies on a publicly available set of Reddit user comments and show that our interpolation strategies deliver a 5.2% perplexity lift. Finally, we describe methods for handling the crucial edge case of out-of-vocabulary (OOV) tokens[1].

Specifically, the contributions of this work are:

1. We evaluate several approaches to handle OOV tokens, covering edge cases not discussed in the LM personalization literature.
2. We provide novel analysis and selection of interpolation coefficients for combining global models with user-personalized models.
3. We experimentally analyze trade-offs and evaluate our personalization mechanisms on public data, enabling replication by the research community.

2 Related Work

Language modeling is a critical component for many NLIs, and personalization is a natural direction to improve these interfaces.

Several published works have explored personalization of language models using historical search queries (Jaech and Ostendorf, 2018), features garnered from social graphs (Wen et al., 2012; Tseng

* Indicates equal contributions

[1] To the best knowledge of the authors, these edge cases are not clearly defined in the literature when combining two LMs trained on two different datasets.

Proceedings of the First Workshop on Natural Language Interfaces, pages 20–26
July 10, 2020.
https://doi.org/10.18653/v1/P17

et al., 2015; Lee et al., 2016), and transfer learning techniques (Yoon et al., 2017). Other work has explored using profile information (location, name, etc.) as additional features to condition trained models (Shokouhi, 2013; Jaech and Ostendorf, 2018). Specifically, in the NLI domain, Google Smart Compose (Chen et al., 2019) productized the approach described in (Chen et al., 2015) by using a linear interpolation of a general background model and a personalized n-gram model to personalize LM predictions in the email authoring setting. We view our work as a natural extension to this line of research because strategies that improve personalization at the language modeling level drive results at the user interface level.

3 Personalized Interpolation Model

The goal of text prediction is strongly aligned with language modeling. The task of language modeling is to predict which words come next, given a set of context words. In this paper, we explore using a combination of both large scale neural LMs and small scale personalized n-gram LMs. This combination has been studied in the literature (Chen et al., 2015) and has been found to be performant. We describe mechanisms for extending this previous work in this section. Once trained, we compute the perplexity of these models not by exponentiation of the cross entropy, but rather by explicitly predicting the probability of test sequences. In practice this model is to be used to rerank sentence completion sequences. As a result, it is impossible to ignore the observation of OOV tokens.

3.1 Personalized n-gram LMs

Back-off n-gram LMs (Kneser and Ney, 1995) have been widely adopted given their simplicity, and efficient parameter estimation and discounting algorithms further improve robustness (Chen et al., 2015). Compared with DNN-based models, n-gram LMs are computationally cheap to train, lightweight to store and query, and fit well even on small data—crucial benefits for personalization. Addressing the sharp distributions and sparse data issues in n-gram counts is critical. We rely on Modified Kneser-Ney smoothing (James, 2000), which is generally accepted as one of the most effective smoothing techniques.

3.2 Global LSTM

For large scale language modeling, neural network methods can produce dramatic improvements in predictive performance (Jozefowicz et al., 2016). Specifically, we use LSTM cells (Hochreiter and Schmidhuber, 1997), known for their ability to capture long distance context without vanishing gradients. By computing the softmax function on the output scores of the LSTM we can extract the LSTM's per-token approximation as language model probabilities.

3.3 Evaluation

We use perplexity (PP) to evaluate the performance of our LMs. PP is a measure of how well a probability model predicts a sample, i.e., how well an LM predicts the next word. This can be treated as a branching factor. Mathematically, PP is the exponentiation of the entropy of a probability distribution. Lower PP is indicative of a better LM. We define lift in perplexity (PP lift) as

$$\text{PP lift} = \frac{PP_{\text{global}} - PP_{\text{interpolated}}}{PP_{\text{global}}}, \quad (1)$$

where $PP_{\text{interpolated}}$ is the perplexity of the interpolated model and PP_{global} is the perplexity of the global LSTM model, which serves as the baseline. Higher PP lift is indicative of a better LM.

3.4 Interpolation Strategies

Past work (Chen et al., 2015) has described mechanisms for interpolating global models with personalized models for each user. Our experimentation mixes a global LSTM model with the personalized n-gram models detailed above[2].

The interpolation is a linear combination of the predicted token probabilities:

$$P = \alpha P_{\text{personal}} + (1 - \alpha) P_{\text{global}} \quad (2)$$

α indicates how much personalization is added to the global model. We explore constant values of α, either globally or for each user. We compute a set of oracle α values, the values of α per user that empirically minimize interpolated perplexity. We compare our strategies for tuning α to these oracle α values, which present the best possible performance on the given user data in Section 5.3. Intuitively, users whose comments have a high proportion of tokens outside the global vocabulary will

[2]We further detail the hyperparameters and training scheme of our LSTM and n-gram models in the appendices.

need more input from the global model than their own personalized model to accurately model their language habits. Thus, we also explore an inverse relationship between α and each user's OOV rate.

3.5 OOV Mitigation Strategies

When training on datasets with a large proportion of OOV tokens, low PP may not indicate a good model. Specifically, if the proportion of OOV tokens in the data is high, the model may assign too much mass to OOV tokens resulting in a model with a propensity to predict the OOV token. Such a model may have low PP, but only because it frequently predicts the commonly occurring OOV token. While this may be an effective model of the pure sequence of tokens, it does not align with downstream objectives present at the interface level which relies on a robust prediction of non-OOV tokens. Because of this disconnect between model and overall task objective, mitigation strategies must be implemented in order to adequately evaluate the performance of LMs in high OOV settings. We evaluate the following strategies to mitigate this behavior:

1. Do nothing, assigning OOV tokens their estimated probabilities;
2. Skip the OOV tokens, scoring only those items known in the training vocabulary; and
3. Back-off to a uniform OOV penalty, assigning a fixed probability ϕ to model the likelihood of selecting the OOV token[3].

When reporting our results we denote PP_{base} as PP observed when using strategy 1, PP_{skip} as PP observed when using strategy 2, and $\text{PP}_{\text{backoff}}$ as PP observed when using strategy 3.

4 Data

The data for our model comes from comments made by users on the Internet social media website Reddit[4]. Reddit is a rich source of natural-language data with high linguistic diversity due to posts about a variety of topics, informality of language, and sheer volume of data. As a linguistic resource, Reddit comments present in a heavily conversational and colloquial tone, and users frequently use slang and misspell words. Because of this there are a high number of unique tokens. As developers of a machine learning system, we seek to balance having a large vocabulary in order to capture the most data with having a small vocabulary in order to keep the model from overfitting. We construct our vocabulary by empirically selecting the n most common tokens observed by randomly selecting Reddit user comments. We then share this vocabulary, created from the global training set, in both the personalized and global models. This value of n must be tuned based on data. When choosing a size for vocabulary, there exists a tradeoff between performance and capturing varied language. Larger vocabularies adversely impact performance but may encapsulate more variability of language. For a given vocabulary size chosen from training data for the global LSTM, we plot the resulting OOV rates for users. As can be seen when comparing Figure 1 and Figure 2, very few gains in user-level OOV rates are seen when expanding the vocabulary size twenty-fold. Thus, we choose a vocabulary size of 50,000.

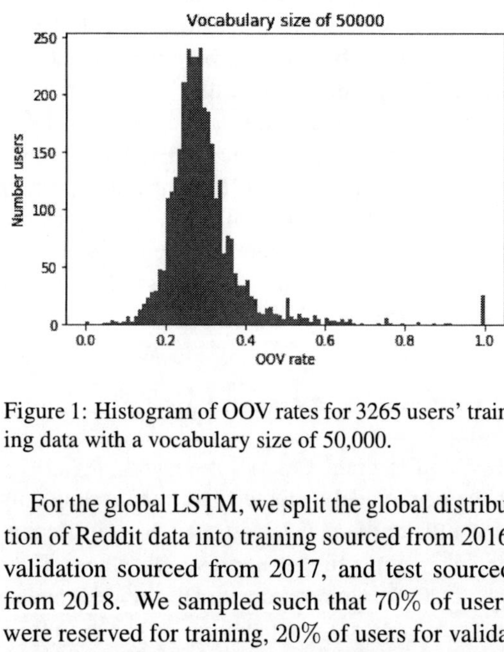

Figure 1: Histogram of OOV rates for 3265 users' training data with a vocabulary size of 50,000.

For the global LSTM, we split the global distribution of Reddit data into training sourced from 2016, validation sourced from 2017, and test sourced from 2018. We sampled such that 70% of users were reserved for training, 20% of users for validation, and 10% of users for test. We allot 100,000 users for the test set and scale the number of users in the other sets accordingly. There are 10 billion total tokens in the training data, with 29 million unique tokens. 90% of unique tokens occur 6 or fewer times, and half of users have 20 or fewer comments per year with an average comment length of

[3] We consider ϕ to be a hyperparameter which must be tuned for each use case. In our experiments we assign ϕ to be $\frac{1}{V}$, where V is the vocabulary size.

[4] We retrieved copies of www.reddit.com user comments from https://pushshift.io/.

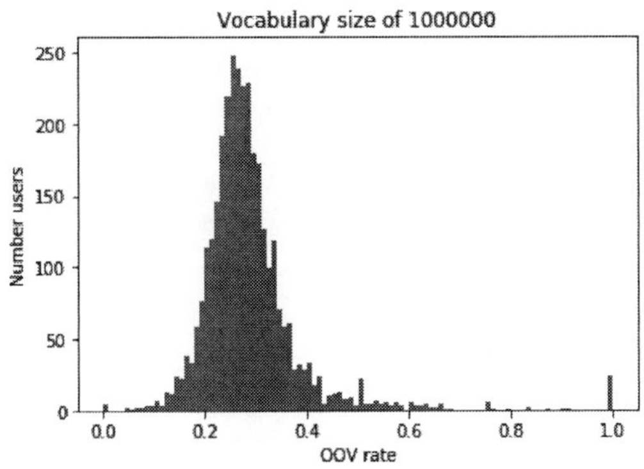

Figure 2: Histogram of OOV rates for 3265 users' training data with a vocabulary size of 1,000,000.

13 tokens. For the personalized n-grams, we selected all comment data from 3265 random Reddit users[6] who made at least one comment in each of 2016, 2017, and 2018. Then, for each user, we selected the data from 2016 as training data, the data from 2017 as validation data, and the data from 2018 as testing data.

5 Results

Here we discuss the results observed when evaluating the interpolated global LSTM and user-personalized n-gram model on users' comments using various OOV mitigation and α interpolation strategies.

5.1 OOV Mitigation Strategies

In our data used for personalization, 68% users have more than 25% OOV rate for validation data, and 65% users have more than 25% OOV rate for training data. This empirically causes large deviations between the different $PP_{backoff}$, PP_{skip}, and PP_{base}. We find that a personalized n-gram model can't handle OOV tokens very well in high OOV settings, because it assigns higher probabilities to OOV tokens than some of the tokens in the vocabulary. As discussed in Section 3.5 high OOV rates at the per-user level PP_{base} present a view of the results that is disconnected from downstream use in an NLI. At the same time, PP_{skip} presents the view most aligned with the downstream task because in an NLI the OOV token should never be shown. However, PP_{skip} comes with some mathematical baggage. Specifically, when all tokens are OOV, the PP_{skip} will be infinite. These two approaches represent the extremes of the strategies which could be used. We argue that $PP_{backoff}$ represents the best of both worlds.

Figure 3 shows that $PP_{backoff}$ provides measurements near the minima that are closely aligned with PP_{skip} while also being free of the mathematical and procedural issues associated with PP_{skip} and PP_{base}. We provide an example to further illustrate the above statement. Consider a high OOV rate comment such as "re-titled jaff ransomware only fivnin." with OOV tokens *re-titled, jaff, ransomware, fivnin.* Following encoding, the mode would see this sequence as "OOV OOV OOV only OOV". When measuring the probability of this sequence a model evaluated using PP_{base} would have lower perplexity because it has been trained to overweight the probability of OOV tokens as they occur more frequently than the tokens they represent. However, this sequence should have far lower probability, and thus higher perplexity, because the model is in fact failing to adequately model the true sequence. We argue that assigning a uniform value θ to OOV tokens will more accurately represent the performance of the model when presented with data with a high quantity of OOV tokens.

Because we believe that $PP_{backoff}$ presents the most accurate picture of model performance, we have chosen to present our results in Section 5.2 and 5.3 using $PP_{backoff}$.

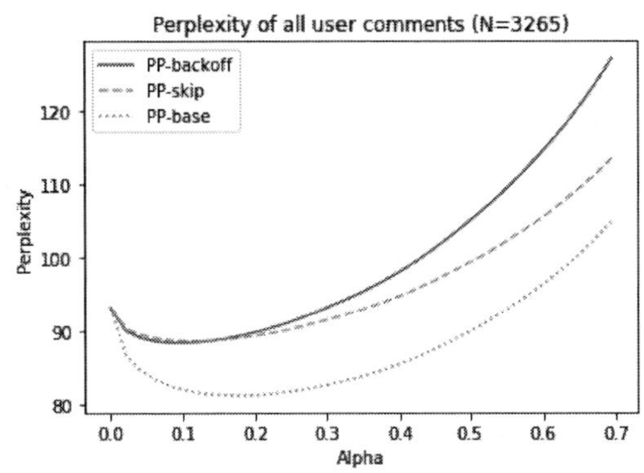

Figure 3: Average of interpolated PP for all users for varied values of $\alpha \leq 0.7$ for each method of approaching OOV tokens.

5.2 Analysis of Personalization

We next present an interesting dichotomy in Figure 4 not previously discussed in the personalization literature. In the constant α for all users setting we can optimize to either minimize the overall $PP_{backoff}$ for all users or to maximize the average $PP_{backoff}$ lift across users. These two objectives result in different constant α^5. Specifically, minimizing PP_{backoff} over users yields $\alpha = 0.105$, providing an improvement for 67.3% of users and an average PP_{backoff} lift of 2.5%. Maximizing the average PP_{backoff} lift per user yields $\alpha = 0.041$, providing an improvement for 74.2% of users and an average PP_{backoff} lift of 2.7%[6].

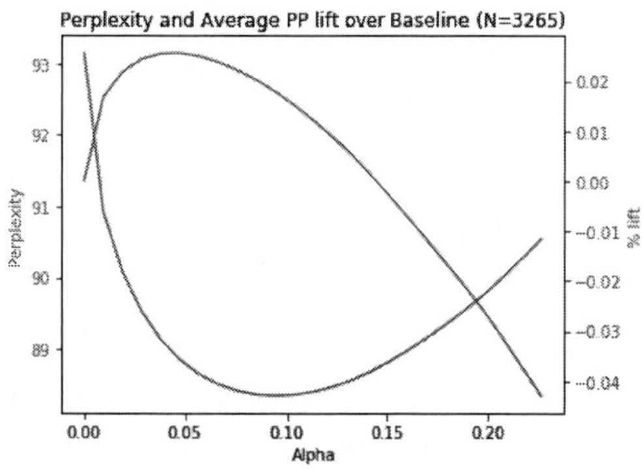

Figure 4: PP_{backoff} and average PP_{backoff} lift over baseline for various values of $\alpha < 0.22$.

5.3 Constant and Personalized Interpolation Coefficient α Optimization

When searching for a constant value for α for all users, $\alpha = 0.105$ achieves the minimum mean interpolated PP_{backoff}, with an average PP_{backoff} lift of 2.5%.

Next, we personalize the value of α for each user. We first produce a set of oracles[6] as described in Section 3.4. With this set of oracle values of α, the average PP_{backoff} lift is 6.1% with the best average PP_{backoff} achievable in this context. While it is possible to compute the oracle values for each user in a production setting, this may not be tractable when user counts are high and there exist latency constraints.

Thus, we try an inverse linear relationship: $\alpha = k \cdot (1 - \text{OOV rate})$. To illustrate the effect of this relationship, we perform this optimization 10 times, using a different random subset of users each time to optimize k and then evaluate on the rest of the users. On average, we observe a PP_{backoff} lift of 5.2%, and 80.1% of users achieve an improvement in PP_{backoff}. In Figure 5 we see that a heuristic approach of lower complexity achieves near-oracle performance, with the distribution of PP_{backoff} for this method closely matching the oracle distribution of PP_{backoff}. We also find that this method of α personalization yields lower PP_{backoff} for more users than using a constant value for α.

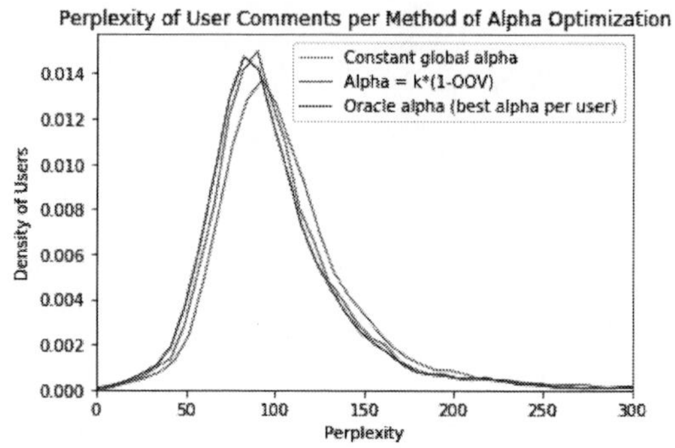

Figure 5: Distribution of interpolated PP_{backoff} for users using each method of α optimization. The values for $\alpha = k \cdot (1 - \text{OOV rate})$ are averaged over 10 random selections.

6 Conclusion & Future Work

In this paper we presented new strategies for interpolating personalized LMs, discussed strategies for handling OOV tokens to give better vision into model performance, and evaluated these strategies on public data allowing the research community to build upon these results. Furthermore, two directions could be worth exploring: Investigate on when personalization is useful at a user level to better interpret the results; Research on user-specific vocabularies for personalized models instead of using a shared vocabulary for both the personalized and global background models.

As NLIs move closer to the user, personalization mechanisms will need to become more robust. We believe the results we have presented form a natural step in building that robustness.

Acknowledgments

We would like to thank the Microsoft Search, Assistant and Intelligence team, and in particular Geisler Antony, Kalyan Ayloo, Mikhail Kulikov, Vipul Agarwal, Anton Amirov, Nick Farn and Kunho Kim, for their invaluable help and support in this research. We also thank T. J. Hazen, Vijay Ramani, and the anonymous reviewers for their insightful feedback and suggestions.

[5]There may be other trade-offs to examine.

[6]Further details are included in the appendices.

References

Lik Harry Chen, Adam John Cheyer, Didier Rene Guzzoni, and Thomas Robert Gruber. 2014. Personalized vocabulary for digital assistant. US Patent 8,903,716.

Mia Xu Chen, Benjamin N Lee, Gagan Bansal, Yuan Cao, Shuyuan Zhang, Justin Lu, Jackie Tsay, Yinan Wang, Andrew M Dai, Zhifeng Chen, et al. 2019. Gmail smart compose: Real-time assisted writing. In *Proceedings of the 25th ACM SIGKDD International Conference on Knowledge Discovery & Data Mining*, pages 2287–2295.

Xie Chen, Xunying Liu, Mark JF Gales, and Philip C Woodland. 2015. Investigation of back-off based interpolation between recurrent neural network and n-gram language models. In *2015 IEEE Workshop on Automatic Speech Recognition and Understanding (ASRU)*, pages 181–186. IEEE.

Sepp Hochreiter and Jürgen Schmidhuber. 1997. Long short-term memory. *Neural computation*, 9(8):1735–1780.

Yuka Ishikawa. 2015. Gender differences in vocabulary use in essay writing by university students. *Procedia-Social and Behavioral Sciences*, 192:593–600.

Aaron Jaech and Mari Ostendorf. 2018. Personalized language model for query auto-completion. *arXiv preprint arXiv:1804.09661*.

Frankie James. 2000. Modified kneser-ney smoothing of n-gram models. *Research Institute for Advanced Computer Science, Tech. Rep. 00.07*.

Rafal Jozefowicz, Oriol Vinyals, Mike Schuster, Noam Shazeer, and Yonghui Wu. 2016. Exploring the limits of language modeling.

Reinhard Kneser and Hermann Ney. 1995. Improved backing-off for m-gram language modeling. In *1995 International Conference on Acoustics, Speech, and Signal Processing*, volume 1, pages 181–184. IEEE.

Hung-Yi Lee, Bo-Hsiang Tseng, Tsung-Hsien Wen, and Yu Tsao. 2016. Personalizing recurrent-neural-network-based language model by social network. *IEEE/ACM Transactions on Audio, Speech, and Language Processing*, 25(3):519–530.

Lee Morse. 2008. System and method for personalizing the user interface of audio rendering devices. US Patent App. 11/779,256.

Hadi Partovi, Roderick Steven Brathwaite, Angus Macdonald Davis, Michael S McCue, Brandon William Porter, John Giannandrea, Eckart Walther, Anthony Accardi, and Zhe Li. 2005. Method and apparatus for content personalization over a telephone interface with adaptive personalization. US Patent 6,842,767.

Ella Rabinovich, Yulia Tsvetkov, and Shuly Wintner. 2018. Native language cognate effects on second language lexical choice. *Transactions of the Association for Computational Linguistics*, 6:329–342.

Alec Radford, Jeffrey Wu, Rewon Child, David Luan, Dario Amodei, and Ilya Sutskever. 2019. Language models are unsupervised multitask learners. *OpenAI Blog*, 1(8):9.

Milad Shokouhi. 2013. Learning to personalize query auto-completion. In *Proceedings of the 36th international ACM SIGIR conference on Research and development in information retrieval*, pages 103–112.

Bo-Hsiang Tseng, Hung-yi Lee, and Lin-Shan Lee. 2015. Personalizing universal recurrent neural network language model with user characteristic features by social network crowdsourcing. In *2015 IEEE Workshop on Automatic Speech Recognition and Understanding (ASRU)*, pages 84–91. IEEE.

Tsung-Hsien Wen, Hung-Yi Lee, Tai-Yuan Chen, and Lin-Shan Lee. 2012. Personalized language modeling by crowd sourcing with social network data for voice access of cloud applications. In *2012 IEEE Spoken Language Technology Workshop (SLT)*, pages 188–193. IEEE.

Seunghyun Yoon, Hyeongu Yun, Yuna Kim, Gyu-tae Park, and Kyomin Jung. 2017. Efficient transfer learning schemes for personalized language modeling using recurrent neural network. In *Workshops at the Thirty-First AAAI Conference on Artificial Intelligence*.

A Appendices

A.1 Hyperparameters and Model Training

The global LSTM model trained token embeddings of size 300, and had hidden unit layers of size 256 and 128, an output projection of dimension 100, and a vocabulary of 50,000 tokens. It was trained with dropout using the Adam optimizer, and we parallel-trained our global LSTM on an Azure[7] Standard_NC24s_v2 machine which includes 24 vCPUs and 4 NVIDIA Tesla P100 GPUs.

The personalized n-gram models were 3-gram modified Kneser-Ney smoothed models with discounting values of 0.5 (1-grams), 1 (2-grams), and 1.5 (3-grams).

A.2 User Analysis Plots

The average size of the user-personalized corpus is around 140 comments, while the median size is 23 comments. The average comment length for each user is around 14 tokens.

[7] www.azure.com

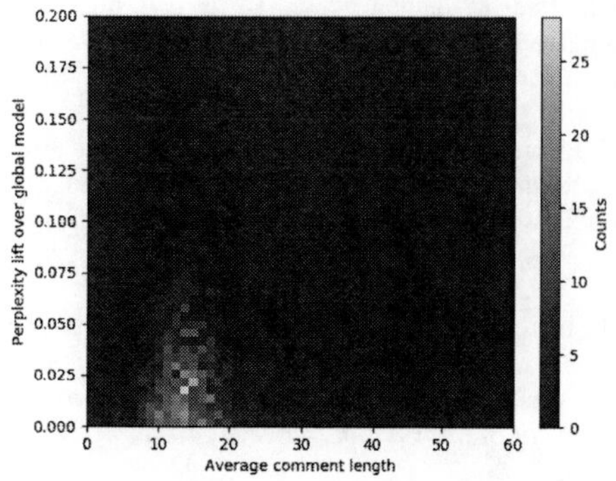

Figure 6: Histogram of PP lift over global model vs. average comment length ($\alpha = 0.105$).

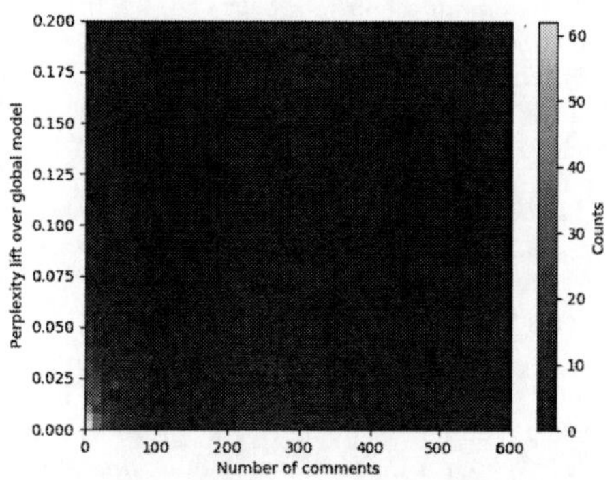

Figure 7: Histogram of PP lift over global model vs. number of comments ($\alpha = 0.105$).

By analyzing the results with the lowest interpolated $PP_{backoff}$ ($\alpha = 0.105$ for all users), we make two observations: users with average comment length less than around 30 tokens don't get much benefit from personalization, and users with less than around 100 comments don't get much benefit from personalization.

A.3 Oracle α Distribution

Figure 8 shows the distribution of the empirically-computed "oracle" values for α.

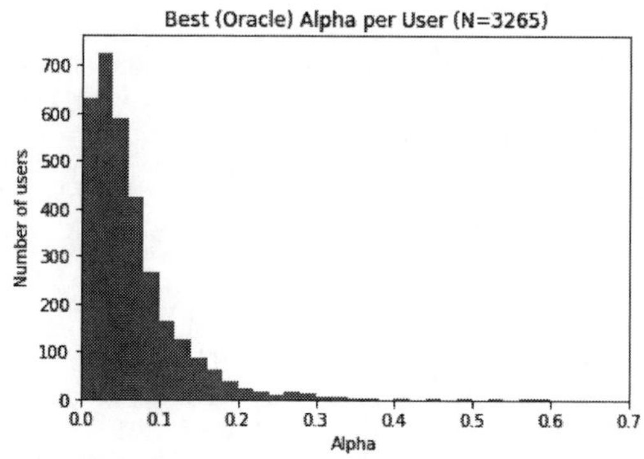

Figure 8: Distribution of oracle values of α per user.

Efficient Deployment of Conversational Natural Language Interfaces over Databases

Anthony Colas*, **Trung Bui**†, **Franck Dernoncourt**†, **Moumita Sinha**†, **Doo Soon Kim**†
University of Florida*, Adobe Research†
acolas1@ufl.edu*,
{bui, franck.dernoncourt, mousinha, dkim}@adobe.com†

Abstract

Many users communicate with chatbots and AI assistants in order to help them with various tasks. A key component of the assistant is the ability to understand and answer a user's natural language questions for question-answering (QA). Because data can be usually stored in a structured manner, an essential step involves turning a natural language question into its corresponding query language. However, in order to train most natural language-to-query-language state-of-the-art models, a large amount of training data is needed first. In most domains, this data is not available and collecting such datasets for various domains can be tedious and time-consuming. In this work, we propose a novel method for accelerating the training dataset collection for developing the natural language-to-query-language machine learning models. Our system allows one to generate conversational multi-term data, where multiple turns define a dialogue session, enabling one to better utilize chatbot interfaces. We train two current state-of-the-art NL-to-QL models, on both an SQL and SPARQL-based datasets in order to showcase the adaptability and efficacy of our created data.

1 Introduction

Chatbots and AI task assistants are widely used today to help users with their everyday needs. One use for these assistants is asking them questions on various areas of knowledge or how to accomplish different tasks (Braun et al., 2017; Cui et al., 2017). Because data is usually stored in a structured database, in order to answer a user's questions, it is essential that the system should first understand the question, and convert it into a structured language query, such as SQL or SPARQL, to fetch the correct answer.

While much research has focused on translating natural languages into query languages (Ngonga Ngomo et al., 2013; Braun et al., 2017; Dubey et al., 2016; Giordani and Moschitti, 2009; Finegan-Dollak et al., 2018; Giordani, 2008; Xu et al., 2017; Zhong et al., 2017), the state-of-the-art systems typically involve a large amount of training data. Therefore, in order to fully utilize these models that translate a natural language (NL) question into query language (QL), one would need to collect large amounts of both NL-QL pairs. Although there are works which involve the collection of NL-QL pairs in different domains (Hemphill et al., 1990; Zelle and Mooney, 1996; Zhong et al., 2017; Yu et al., 2018, 2019b), data is still not available in most domains, and thus this collection process can be both time-consuming and expensive.

Natural Language	Query Language (SQL)
Turn 1: Who are the employees that work in the IT department and have the last name Smith?	***Turn 1***:`SELECT name FROM Employees WHERE last_name = 'Smith' AND dept_name = 'IT';`
Turn 2: How many of them started working after Jan 1, 2020?	***Turn 2***:`SELECT Count(name) FROM Employees WHERE last_name = 'Smith' AND dept_name = 'IT' AND hire_date > '01-01-2020';`
Turn 3: *What are their phone numbers?*	***Turn 3***:`SELECT phone_number FROM Employees WHERE last_name = 'Smith' AND dept_name = 'IT' AND hire_data > '01-01-2020';`

Figure 1: Example illustrating a three-turn dialogue, featuring the natural language (first column) and query language (second column) representations.

In this work, we address the problem of having insufficient data collection methodologies by proposing a novel approach that accelerates the data collection process for use in NL-to-QL models. Additionally, our approach focuses on generating conversation data, where the context of a dialogue turn is used to generate a subsequent pair. In this way, we better simulate the data necessary for real world chatbots and voice assistants, as exemplified in Figure 1. Our contributions are as follows:

Proceedings of the First Workshop on Natural Language Interfaces, pages 27–36
July 10, 2020.
https://doi.org/10.18653/v1/P17

- We develop a novel approach that accelerates the creation of NL-to-QL data pairs. Primarily, our approach tackles the problem in the conversational domain.
- We showcase our data collection system on two different QLs, SQL and SPARQL, demonstrating the flexibility of our system.
- Finally, we demonstrate the use of current single-turn state-of-the-art approaches on these two domains to prove the adaptability of our system to current models.

Though our data collection implementation focuses on conversational data, the models we deploy are single-turn. Our main focus here is to give a demonstration of the generated data. Section 3 and Section 4 show the adaptability of our data collection scheme to these kinds of models.

The rest of this paper is structured as follows: Section 2 surveys prior work in both the NL-to-QL and data collection space, Section 3 details our novel conversational data collection approach, Section 4 walks through examples in both the SQL and SPARQL domain, Section 5 describes the current models we have trained and tested on the generated data, Section 6 gives the results on the data and models, and Section 7 concludes our work.

2 Related Work

In the field of natural language interfaces for structured data there are bodies of work that 1) focus on translating natural language to a specific query language and that 2) relate to collecting semantic parsing data for natural language interfaces.

2.1 NL-to-QL

NL-to-QL models have worked to transform natural language queries into their respective logical form (LF) representations (Dong and Lapata, 2016), SQL queries (Xu et al., 2017; Zhong et al., 2017; Finegan-Dollak et al., 2018; Cai et al., 2018), or SPARQL queries (Ngonga Ngomo et al., 2013; Dubey et al., 2016). While work in the SPARQL domain first normalize and match the queries, state-of-the-art work in translating NL to SQL involves neural architectures. Dong and Lapata (2016) utilize and encoder-decoder framework to translate NL questions into their LF representation. Xu et al. (2017) propose a sketch-based model where a neural network predicts each slot of the sketch. The architecture built by Zhong et al. (2017) uses policy-based reinforcement learning in order to translate NL to SQL. While Finegan-Dollak et al. (2018)'s main takeaway is how different evaluations effect the generalization problem in translating NL to SQL, they approach the problem with a seq2seq model. Because of the volume of data needed to fully utilize these models, it can be difficult to adapt to different domains.

In the multi-turn domain, Saha et al. (2018) first approach the problem of complex sequential question-answering (CSQA) by first building a large-scale QA dataset made to answer questions found in Wikidata [1]. However, their data collection process was extremely laborious, as their process required in-house annotators, crowdsourced workers, and multiple iterations. Additionally, their approach was end-to-end, meaning the output was an expected answer. Nevertheless, because their approach incorporate the query representation, we plan to further incorporate their approach into our data collection process in future work.Yu et al. (2019a) also develop the first general-purpose DB querying dialogue system. However, their system dialogues focus on clarifying a NL question for user verification, before returning an answer. Our work focuses on generating conversational data about specific database entities and properties.

2.2 Data Collection for Semantic Parsing

NL question semantic parsers have been developed for single-turn QA in order to translate simple NL questions into their respective LFs (Wang et al., 2015). In their approach, Wang et al. (2015) first begin with a *domain*, building a seed lexicon of that domain. Next, they find the LF and canonical utterance templates corresponding based on the lexicon. Wang et al. (2015) then paraphrase their canonical utterances via crowd-sourcing. Iyer et al. (2017) learn a semantic parser via an encoder-decoder model by using NL/SQL templates. This model is tuned through user feedback, where incorrect queries are annotated by crowd-workers. Paraphrasing is accomplished through the Paraphrasing Database (PPDB) (Ganitkevitch et al., 2013).

While the two previously mentioned works are single-turn semantic parsers, Shah et al. (2018) develop a multi-turn semantic parser. Their approach begins with a task schema and API which is used to create dialogue outlines for the provided domain.

[1]https://www.wikidata.org/wiki/Wikidata:Main_Page

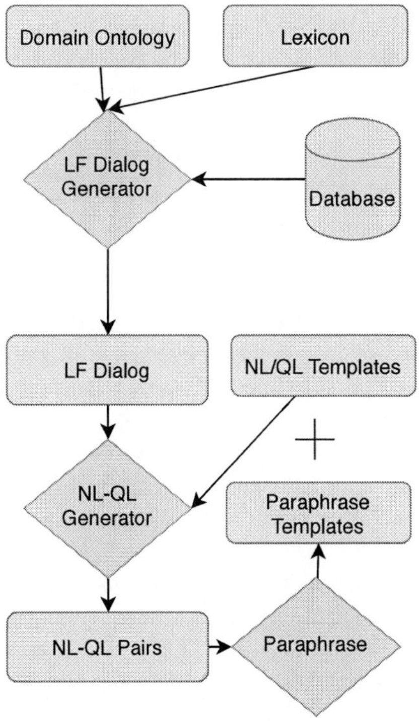

Figure 2: An overview of our conversational data collection deployment system. Blue shapes denote the input/output data at each stage, while green diamonds denote the processes of the system. The "plus" sign denotes the concatenation of both seed templates and paraphrase templates.

These dialogue outlines involve a user and system bot that simulate a scenario. The dialogues are then paraphrased via crowd-sourcing. However, Shah et al. (2018) use the logical-form representation of the utterances rather than their query language representation. In our work, we re-incorporate the paraphrases into the dialogue generation phase.

3 Data Collection System

Our conversational data collection strategy is developed to efficiently collect NL/QL pairs for training data in models which translate the NL into QL in a multi-turn setting. Because domain data is required when training a chatbot to query a database when converting from NL to QL, our approach is generalized so that one can easily collect data for their respective domain.

3.1 Overview

Our approach in collecting data is made of the four following steps: 1) First we generate the dialogue represented as LFs, forming the abstract representations of NL questions, 2) Next, we convert the LFs into an NL template and QL templates 3) We then collect paraphrases of the natural language templates, and 4) Finally, we use these paraphrases to further develop our dialog generator. In generating our dialogue, the context of each previous turn is taken in order to develop the current turn. Figure 2 presents our data deployment system. We divide and expand upon the steps further in the next sections.

3.2 Definitions

We first define the following notations in our data collection system:

- U_n: an utterance in the dialogue.
- LF_n: the LF *n* in the dialogue.
- NL_n: the NL utterance corresponding to LF_n.
- QL_n: the QL utterance corresponding to LF_n.

3.3 Input Module

The input to our data collection system consists of a domain ontology, lexicon, and database. These should be provided by the user and vary depending on the type of data one requires. The domain ontology defines the *<object, relation, property>* triples of a given dataset, where each object has a set of properties connected through a relation, e.g. *<ACL 2020, has_location, Seattle>*. The lexicon file defines each data field, along with its NL and QL representation, important in the NL-QL Generator step. The database is the data in structured form.

3.4 Logical Form Dialogue Generator

In order to appropriately simulate a conversation between a user and chatbot, the synthetic dialogue must first be generated. This is done by first outlining the dialog via LFs, where the system generates, LF_{1-n}. These outlines are an abstract but understandable representation of the dialogue taking into account the type, entity, and relation of a question. Thus, our parser builds a dialogue based on a domain ontology, lexicon, and domain database.

The LFs take the form of three predicates: *Retrieve-Objects*, *Inquire-Property*, and *Compute*, each taking on their own arguments. For the *Retrieve-Objects* predicate, the LF fetches an instance that satisfies a condition. As arguments,

Retrieve-Objects takes an *entity type*, $\mathbf{t_n^i}$ from the ontology, a boolean *condition* $\mathbf{c_n^i}$, and a *property value*,$\mathbf{p_n^i}$, from the DB. For the *Inquire-Property* predicate, given an *anchor entity* $\mathbf{ae_n^i}$, *target instance*, $\mathbf{ti_n^i}$, and an *inference path* $\mathbf{ip_n^i}$ from the entity to that instance, the LF finds the property in that path of the anchor entity. The *Compute* predicate denotes a *computation* $\mathbf{comp_n^i}$ over a set of given objects, thus its arguments are comprised of *Retrieve-Objects* arguments and an operation to be performed. [2]. For our work, we focus on using the *COUNT* aggregate function. Future work can easily adapt more aggregate functions into our model such as *MAX* or *MIN* depending on the values contained in the database.

More formally, each LF can be described as follows:

$$\begin{aligned} \boldsymbol{LF_n} \rightarrow \{&Retrieve-Objects(t_n^i, c_n^i, p_n^i),\\ &Inquire-Property(ae_n^i, ti_n^i, ip_n^i),\\ &Compute(comp_n^i, t_n^i, c_n^i, p_n^i)\} \end{aligned} \quad (1)$$

At the start of a dialogue, a random LF predicate is selected, given the database schema, lexicon, and domain ontology. The subsequent turns in the dialogue are built conditionally on the previous turn. Therefore, given a LF_{n-1}, when generating LF_n the context of LF_{n-1} is further taken into consideration including its arguments, type, and answer. The subsequent predicate is also chosen at random, however its values are conditional on the arguments and answer(s) of the current predicate. For example, if LF_{n-1} is an *Retrieve-Objects* predicate and another *Retrieve-Objects* predicate is chosen as LF_n, this LF can further filter the answer of LF_{n-1} by using an additional condition. Table 1 summarizes the types of LFs, along with an explanation and example of each both in LF and NL, which we discuss in the next section.

3.5 NL-QL Generator

Once the LF generator is complete, the data collection system generates an NL utterance along with its corresponding QL. To generate such pairs, the NL-QL generator takes in each LF from the LF Dialog as input. Based on the predicate type, an NL-QL pair is selected and filled with corresponding arguments of the predicate. Thus, the system uses NL seed templates for the *Retrieve-Objects*, *Inquire-Property*, and *Compute* predicates to create the initial training data for the conversational dialogue. For example, one NL template for turns after NL_1 can be *"How about <entity>?"*

The aforementioned seed templates are hand-crafted based on the type of data and are thus left to the user to create. These data are hand-crafted to increase the quality of the seed templates in terms of coherency and utility, important features not only for quality training data, but also when performing the paraphrase task. Because we hand-crafted the query language templates, we also guarantee that the queries are executable for their corresponding QLs, SQL or SPARQL in this work. For the QL, we fill in slots for field names, aliases, and values, utilizing the information in the domain ontology, lexicon, and database schema. Note, 'field' refers to column names in relational DBs (queried with SQL) and type names in graph DBs (queried with SPARQL). To reiterate, the NL-QL generator takes each LF_n, with its respective arguments, and seed templates as input, and outputs a $NL_n - QL_n$ pair, where $U_n \rightarrow (NL_n, QL_n)$. Section 4 goes through detailed examples of various NL-QL pairs.

3.6 Paraphrase

The final step involves the paraphrasing of the seed NL templates given in the NL-QL Generator step. To paraphrase the seed NL templates, we first provide crowdworkers from Amazon Mechanical Turk (AMT) [3] with the instantiated templates, the output from the first iteration of the NL-QL generator. We ask the workers to paraphrase the seed templates while keeping the meaning/intent of the original questions. After collecting these paraphrased questions, we further abstract them and link them to their respective predicate representation. In this way, the paraphrases can be utilized in further iterations of the NL-QL Generator step and instantiated when generating new dialogues for training data. While abstracting the templates, we manually scan them for quality control purposes. Furthermore, we ran multiple trial runs in presenting the problem to the AMT workers. Previous work (Wang et al., 2015; Shah et al., 2018) also use similar crowdsourcing techniques in order to paraphrase their templates. Via AMT, Wang et al. (2015) paraphrase canonical utterance, natural language representations to single-turn LFs, while Shah et al. (2018) paraphrase dialogue outlines as their final step.

[2]**n** refers to the dialogue turn, while **i** refers to the number of dialogue generated.

[3]https://www.mturk.com/

Predicate	Explanation	Example	LF
Retrieve-Objects	Gets objects from DB	Which employees have building no. equal to 5?	Retrieve-Objects(employee(ALL), (employee.building_no,'=',5))
Inquire-Property	Gets an object's property	What is the office of James?	Inquire-Property(James, office)
Compute	CompuAggregate function	How many employees have hire year equal to 2010?	Compute(COUNT, employee(ALL), [('hire_year', 2010)])

Table 1: LF predicate summary with an explanation and example of each, both in NL and LF.

Similarly to Shah et al. (2018), we input the paraphrases back into our NL-QL generation step. Figure 2 illustrates this through the "+" symbol, signifying that the paraphrases are appended to the seed templates when mapping to LF and creating the final NL-QL pairs. This approach can take multiple iterations, as the user sees fit to the NL question generation task in their data domain.

4 Data Examples

In this section we will showcase examples in both the SQL and SPARQL domain and traverse through each stage of our Data Collection System. We first begin with SQL, used to query relational databases, and then demonstrate our system with a graph querying language, SPARQL. By doing so, we show the extendability of our approach to various structured QLs. Moreover, we confirm the importance of generating executable queries in a conversational data collection system.

4.1 SQL

Through our data collection system for conversational QA, we are able to produce contextual dependent NL-SQL pairs. For the SQL example, suppose a user wants to produce data for an employee directory relational database. Figure 3 gives an example of possible input files needed to produce this kind of conversational data with our data collection system, including a domain ontology with two entities *Employee* and *Department*, a lexicon to map NL and QL instances, and a database containing *Employee* and *Department* data.

Thus, given the input files in Figure 3, possible LF_n values with each predicate are:

(i) Retrieve-Object(employee(ALL), (employee.dept_name,'=', Marketing))

(ii) Inquire-Property(James,dept_name)

(iii) Computation(COUNT,employee(ALL), [('works_in', 'IT')])

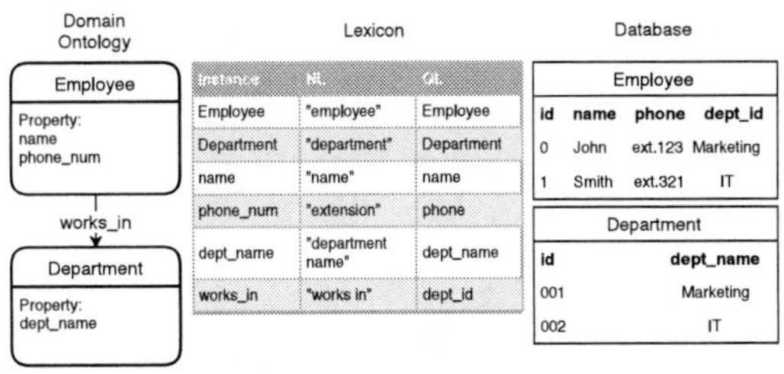

Figure 3: Example ontology schema, lexicon, and database. The two tables in the Database are used throughout our SQL example.

In (i), the logical form represents a retrieval of employee objects who work in the Marketing department. (ii) asks about the department name of James. (iii) computes the total number of employees who work in the IT department. During the generation of LF_1, one of these LFs can be generated. Then for LF_2 - LF_n, the context is passed along to generate the LFs. The n denotes the number of turns a dialogue can take. As an example, given LF_1 is (1) from the aforementioned LFs, LF_2 can be *Inquire-Property(Answer,phone_num)*, where *Answer* denotes the objects returned by LF_1. Our dialogue generation system allows one to tune the number of turns and number of dialogues generated from the given input.

For the NL-QL step, our input includes the dialogues represented as LFs along with NL-QL seed templates described in Section 3.5. Possible templates are given in Table 2. Note, that we refer to a column in a relational DB as a field. Taking our previous *Retrieve-Objects* example, the filled seed template would read: "Which employee have department equal to Marketing?" The Lexicon from Figure 3 is utilized here, as the instance name is mapped to its NL name. Similarly, its QL name (table name) is mapped in the SQL query.

Finally, in the final step, as explained in 3.5, the NL seed templates are paraphrased via crowdsourcing, e.g. "Which employee have department equal to Marketing?" can be paraphrased into "Who works in the marketing department?".

Predicate	Template
Retrieve-Object	Which <entity>have <field name> equal to <instance>?
Inquire-Property	What is the <field name> of <entity value>?
Computation	How many <entity>have <field name>equal to <instance>?

Table 2: Examples of seed templates with their respective predicates. <entity>refers to an entity type. <field name>corresponds to a column in a relational DB or a relation in a graph DB. <instance>refers to the value of that field in the DB. <entity value>is an instance of an entity in the DB.

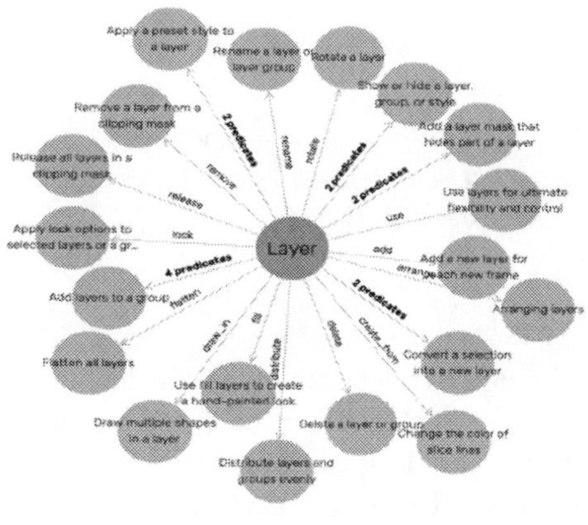

Figure 4: An example of a subgraph in the Photoshop Knowledge Graph. The Layer object (red node), can be seen connected to its objects (blue nodes) through relations. Here we can see that the Layer entity is connected to the various actions connected to "Photoshop Layers", such as "flatten", "lock", and "use", where the object nodes show how they can be performed.

4.2 SPARQL

SPARQL is used to query graph databases, where entities are linked together through relations. These graph databases usually take the form of triples in the form: *<subject,relation,object>*. Because both LF-Generator and NL-QL Generator remain the same as in Section 4.1, here we examine the main differences in the system data when utilizing SPARQL instead of SQL. As a guide, we refer to the example give in Figure 4.

Figure 4 gives an example of a subgraph found in the Photoshop Knowledge Graph (KG). This KG contains the various tools, dialogs, shortcuts, and options found in Photoshop, connected to their options and definitions through relations. The KG is extracted from the Photoshop Wiki. Similarly to the SQL example above, we input a domain ontology, lexicon, and database to the conversational data collection system. However, in the case of a graph database, the entities found in the ontology are more clearly defined in a graph database. Additionally, instead of a table structure, the database is in the form of *<subject,relation,object>* triples, where each entity belongs to a *type* defined in the ontology.

While the the types of LFs generated in the LF-Generator are equivalent, a *property* now refers to the relation found in the triple, while a property refers to the object of a KB triple. For example, an entity such as the one found in figure 4 may have various properties, including "has_shortcut" and "has_option". When generating NL-QL pairs, the generator again takes from the out of the LF-Generator, lexicon, and seed templates, where the QL template is SPARQL-based instead of SQL-based. Paraphrases are collected in the same way. Thus, an example Photoshop Retrieve-Object LF template question, and paraphrase may look like: "LF: Retrieve-Objects(tool(ALL), (tool.has_shortcut, '=', 'H'))", "Template: Which ⟨ entities⟩ have ⟨ relation⟩ equal to ⟨ object⟩?", and "Paraphrase: What's the tool with the H shortcut?"

5 Experiments

We will now examine our experiments with a relational and graph database setting. We first briefly discuss the data used in constructing the converstational dataset and then describe the various models utilized in translating the NL questions into their respective structured queries.

5.1 Data

For our experiments involving SQL data, we construct an NL-QL conversational dataset on data based on a proprietary web analytics tool. In our results table, we refer to this dataset as *Web-Analytics*. For the graph-database, we construct an NL-QL conversational dataset based on the Photoshop KB, as the one exemplified in Section 4.1. As previously noted, this KB contains various entities found in Photoshop, connected to their properties, through predicates which define the properties. In total, the KB contains 15,381 triples, with 3,410 triples that correspond to how-to type queries.

After running our conversational data collection system on both set of data, we collected 288 and 73 NL-QL pairs of templates for the Photoshop

	Photoshop	Web-Analytics
Templates	288	73

Table 3: Number of templates for each dataset, where the Photoshop dataset is SPARQL-based and Web-Analytics dataset is SQL-based.

and Web-Analytics datasets, respectively. Table 3 summarizes these statistics. Additionally, we configured our system to give 3 turn dialogues.

5.2 Models

In our experiments we utilize single-turn NL-QL models. Specifically, we utilize the baselines defined by Finegan-Dollak et al. (2018).

The first baseline is a seq2seq model with attention-based copying, originally proposed by Jia and Liang (2016). This model takes an NL utterance as input and outputs a structured query. Included in the output is a COPY token, which signifies the copying of an input token. In the copying mechanism model, the loss is calculated based on the accumulation of both the probability of distribution of the tokens in the output and the probability of copying from an input token. This copying probability is calculated as the categorical cross entropy of the distributed attention scores across the input's tokens, where the token with the max attention score is chosen as the output token.

The second baseline is a template-based model developed by Finegan-Dollak et al. (2018). This model takes in natural language questions, along with query templates to train. Since our data collection system directly utilizes templates to generate the data, this model is easily adaptable to our setting. We simply use the templates we collect from both the seed-templates and paraphrasing tasks, as well as the slot values extracted from the source DB when creating the dialogue data to train the model. In the template-based model, there are two decisions being made. First the model selects the best template to choose from the input. This is done by passing the final hidden states of a bi-LSTM through a feed-forward neural network. Next, the model selects the words in an input NL-question which can fill the template slots. Again, the same bi-LSTM is used to predict whether an input token is used in the output query or not. Thus, given a natural language question, the model jointly learns the best template from the given input, as well as the values that fill the template's slots. Please note, that while this model is best fitted for our dataset,

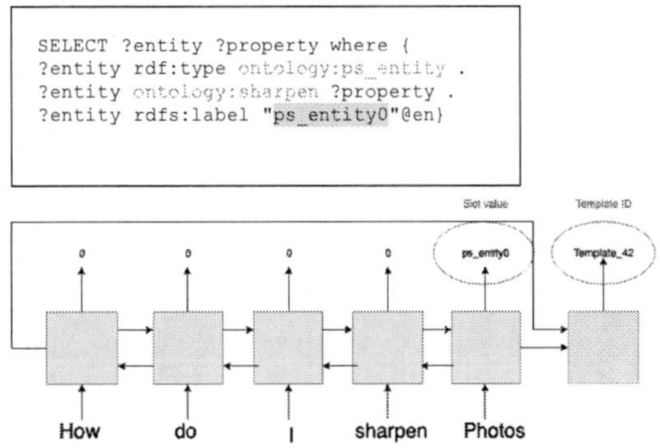

Figure 5: The template-based model developed by Finegan-Dollak et al. (2018), where the blue boxes represent LSTM cells and the green box represents a feed-forward neural network. 'Photos' is classified as a slot value, while the template chosen (Tempalte_42), is depicted above the model. In the template, the entity slot is highlighted in yellow and the properties which make the template unique are in red.

it does not generalize well to data outside of the trained domain due to the template selection task. Figure 5, inspired by Finegan-Dollak et al. (2018), shows an example of the template-based model with our own input in the SPARQL domain.

Although our dataset collection system generates multi-turn data, because of the immaturity of multi-turn NL-to-QL models, we leave the use of multi-turn models for future work. We do however, mention the model developed by Saha et al. (2018), which answers complex sequential natural language questions over KBs, which can be further integrated in future work.

5.3 Settings

We experimented with both the seq2seq and template-based models on the SQL-based and SPARQL-based datasets previously discussed. For the Photoshop SPARQL dataset, we generated *2,100* single-turn data pairs utilizing our data collection system, while generating *3,504* single-data pairs for the web-analytics dataset. Experiments all used a 90/10 train/validation set split.

6 Results

We evaluated the models on our generated datasets for exact-match accuracy of the SQL/SPARQL output queries. The results (shown in Table 4) indicate that in both cases the seq2seq model outperforms the template-based model. While the seq2seq gives an accuracy of .726 and .738, the template-based

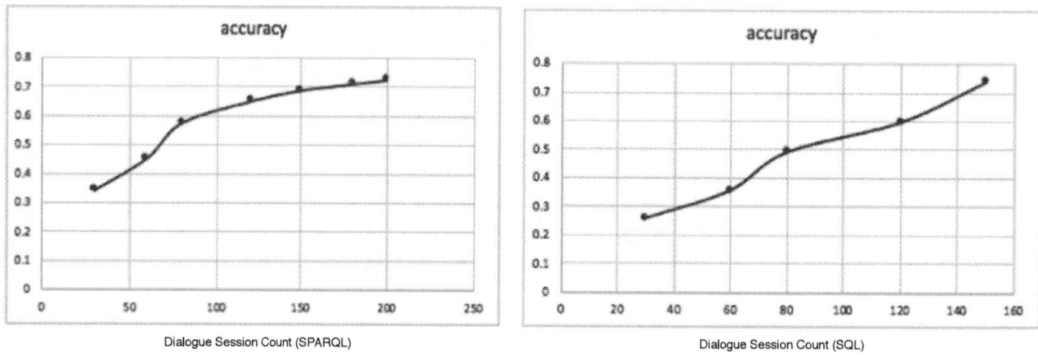

Figure 6: The above graphs show that as the dialogue session count increases for both the Photoshop SPARQL (left) and Web-Analytics SQL (right) dataset, the accuracy also increases. The y-axis of each graph marks the accuracy, while the x-axis marks the number of dialogue sessions for each dataset.

	Photoshop	**Web-Analytics**
Seq2seq	.726	.738
Template-based	.305	.641

Table 4: Results on the accuracy of the NL-to-QL task on the generated single-turn Photoshop and Web-Analytics datasets.

model results in .305 and .641 accuracy. Furthermore, the template-based model performs better on the Web-Analytics SQL-based dataset. This may be because the number of templates contained in the SQL dataset is almost four times greater than the number of templates contained in the Photoshop SPARQL dataset, 73 compared to 288.

We also investigate how the accuracy of the models increase, as the number of samples generated by our data collection system increase. Figure 6 shows that for our best performing model (seq2seq), as the number of dialogue sessions (or data points) increases, the accuracy increases. While this is expected, it also shows that through out dialog creation system, one can improve their NL-to-QL application's performance by configuring the data creation system with more dialogues and templates.

Though the models use synthetic data generated by our system, our system allows one to accelerate the data collection process and quickly deploy an NL-to-QL system that gives reasonably accurate results. This deployed system can then later collect data collected from real application users, where the application logs where a correct or incorrect response may have been returned. Iyer et al. (2017) explore this kind of work which learns from user feedback, where users marked utterances as correct or incorrect, and the accuracy of the semantic parser increased as a result.

7 Conclusion

In this work, we propose a conversational data collection system which accelerates the deployment of conversational natural language interface applications which utilize structured data. We describe the three main processes of our system, including the *LF Dialog Generator*, the *NL-QL Generator*, and the *Paraphrase* component. By taking in a domain ontology, lexicon, and structured database as input, our system generates NL-QL multi-turn pairs which can be used to train systems that translate NL to QL. Each component of our system is examined in both the SQL and SPARQL QL domain. We then validate our data by training state-of-the-art NL to QL models on single-turn utterances. Our experiments show promising results in both the SQL and SPARQL domains, while providing an efficient method to generate data for the development of multi-turn models.

References

Daniel Braun, Adrian Hernandez Mendez, Florian Matthes, and Manfred Langen. 2017. Evaluating natural language understanding services for conversational question answering systems. In *Proceedings of the 18th Annual SIGdial Meeting on Discourse and Dialogue*, pages 174–185.

Ruichu Cai, Boyan Xu, Zhenjie Zhang, Xiaoyan Yang, Zijian Li, and Zhihao Liang. 2018. An encoder-decoder framework translating natural language to database queries. In *Proceedings of the 27th International Joint Conference on Artificial Intelligence*, pages 3977–3983.

Lei Cui, Shaohan Huang, Furu Wei, Chuanqi Tan, Chaoqun Duan, and Ming Zhou. 2017. SuperAgent: A customer service chatbot for e-commerce websites. In *Proceedings of ACL 2017, System Demonstrations*, pages 97–102, Vancouver, Canada. Association for Computational Linguistics.

Li Dong and Mirella Lapata. 2016. Language to logical form with neural attention. In *Proceedings of the 54th Annual Meeting of the Association for Computational Linguistics (Volume 1: Long Papers)*, pages 33–43.

Mohnish Dubey, Sourish Dasgupta, Ankit Sharma, Konrad Höffner, and Jens Lehmann. 2016. Asknow: A framework for natural language query formalization in sparql. In *European Semantic Web Conference*, pages 300–316. Springer.

Catherine Finegan-Dollak, Jonathan K Kummerfeld, Li Zhang, Karthik Ramanathan, Sesh Sadasivam, Rui Zhang, and Dragomir Radev. 2018. Improving text-to-sql evaluation methodology. In *Proceedings of the 56th Annual Meeting of the Association for Computational Linguistics (Volume 1: Long Papers)*, pages 351–360.

Juri Ganitkevitch, Benjamin Van Durme, and Chris Callison-Burch. 2013. Ppdb: The paraphrase database. In *Proceedings of the 2013 Conference of the North American Chapter of the Association for Computational Linguistics: Human Language Technologies*, pages 758–764.

Alessandra Giordani. 2008. Mapping natural language into sql in a nlidb. In *International Conference on Application of Natural Language to Information Systems*, pages 367–371. Springer.

Alessandra Giordani and Alessandro Moschitti. 2009. Semantic mapping between natural language questions and sql queries via syntactic pairing. In *International Conference on Application of Natural Language to Information Systems*, pages 207–221. Springer.

Charles T Hemphill, John J Godfrey, and George R Doddington. 1990. The atis spoken language systems pilot corpus. In *Speech and Natural Language: Proceedings of a Workshop Held at Hidden Valley, Pennsylvania, June 24-27, 1990.*

Srinivasan Iyer, Ioannis Konstas, Alvin Cheung, Jayant Krishnamurthy, and Luke Zettlemoyer. 2017. Learning a neural semantic parser from user feedback. In *Proceedings of the 55th Annual Meeting of the Association for Computational Linguistics (Volume 1: Long Papers)*, pages 963–973.

Robin Jia and Percy Liang. 2016. Data recombination for neural semantic parsing. In *Proceedings of the 54th Annual Meeting of the Association for Computational Linguistics (Volume 1: Long Papers)*, pages 12–22.

Axel-Cyrille Ngonga Ngomo, Lorenz Bühmann, Christina Unger, Jens Lehmann, and Daniel Gerber. 2013. Sorry, i don't speak sparql: translating sparql queries into natural language. In *Proceedings of the 22nd international conference on World Wide Web*, pages 977–988.

Amrita Saha, Vardaan Pahuja, Mitesh M Khapra, Karthik Sankaranarayanan, and Sarath Chandar. 2018. Complex sequential question answering: Towards learning to converse over linked question answer pairs with a knowledge graph. In *Thirty-Second AAAI Conference on Artificial Intelligence.*

Pararth Shah, Dilek Hakkani-Tür, Gokhan Tür, Abhinav Rastogi, Ankur Bapna, Neha Nayak, and Larry Heck. 2018. Building a conversational agent overnight with dialogue self-play. *arXiv preprint arXiv:1801.04871.*

Yushi Wang, Jonathan Berant, and Percy Liang. 2015. Building a semantic parser overnight. In *Proceedings of the 53rd Annual Meeting of the Association for Computational Linguistics and the 7th International Joint Conference on Natural Language Processing (Volume 1: Long Papers)*, pages 1332–1342.

Xiaojun Xu, Chang Liu, and Dawn Song. 2017. Sqlnet: Generating structured queries from natural language without reinforcement learning. *arXiv preprint arXiv:1711.04436.*

Tao Yu, Rui Zhang, Heyang Er, Suyi Li, Eric Xue, Bo Pang, Xi Victoria Lin, Yi Chern Tan, Tianze Shi, Zihan Li, et al. 2019a. Cosql: A conversational text-to-sql challenge towards cross-domain natural language interfaces to databases. In *Proceedings of the 2019 Conference on Empirical Methods in Natural Language Processing and the 9th International Joint Conference on Natural Language Processing (EMNLP-IJCNLP)*, pages 1962–1979.

Tao Yu, Rui Zhang, Kai Yang, Michihiro Yasunaga, Dongxu Wang, Zifan Li, James Ma, Irene Li, Qingning Yao, Shanelle Roman, et al. 2018. Spider: A large-scale human-labeled dataset for complex and cross-domain semantic parsing and text-to-sql task. In *Proceedings of the 2018 Conference on Empirical Methods in Natural Language Processing*, pages 3911–3921.

Tao Yu, Rui Zhang, Michihiro Yasunaga, Yi Chern Tan, Xi Victoria Lin, Suyi Li, Heyang Er, Irene Li, Bo Pang, Tao Chen, et al. 2019b. Sparc: Cross-domain semantic parsing in context. In *Proceedings of the 57th Annual Meeting of the Association for Computational Linguistics*, pages 4511–4523.

John M Zelle and Raymond J Mooney. 1996. Learning to parse database queries using inductive logic programming. In *Proceedings of the national conference on artificial intelligence*, pages 1050–1055.

Victor Zhong, Caiming Xiong, and Richard Socher. 2017. Seq2sql: Generating structured queries from natural language using reinforcement learning. *arXiv preprint arXiv:1709.00103*.

Neural Multi-Task Text Normalization and Sanitization with Pointer-Generator

Van-Hoang Nguyen
Innovation Lab, PayPal
Singapore
vanguyen@paypal.com

Cavallari Sandro
Innovation Lab, PayPal
Singapore
scavallari@paypal.com

Abstract

Text normalization and sanitization are intrinsic components of Natural Language Inferences. In Information Retrieval or Dialogue Generation, normalization of user queries or utterances enhances linguistic understanding by translating non-canonical text to its canonical form, on which many state-of-the-art language models are trained. On the other hand, text sanitization removes sensitive information to guarantee user privacy and anonymity. Existing approaches to normalization and sanitization mainly rely on hand-crafted heuristics and syntactic features of individual tokens while disregarding the linguistic context. Moreover, such context-unaware solutions cannot dynamically determine whether out-of-vocab tokens are misspelt or are entity names. In this work, we formulate text normalization and sanitization as a multi-task text generation approach and propose a neural pointer-generator network based on multi-head attention. Its generator effectively captures linguistic context during normalization and sanitization while its pointer dynamically preserves the entities that are generally missing in the vocabulary. Experiments show that our generation approach outperforms both token-based text normalization and sanitization, while the pointer-generator improves the generator-only baseline in terms of BLEU4 score, and classical attentional pointer networks in terms of pointing accuracy.

1 Introduction

Early Natural Language Processing (NLP) faced the long-standing limitation of human language understanding, mainly due to linguistic morphology or the wide variance of word forms. Therefore, a crucial requirement to obtain outstanding performance for modern NLP systems is the availability of "standardized" textual data (Guyon et al., 1996; Rahm and Do, 2000). Standardizing or normalizing textual data reduces the domain complexity, hence improves the generalization of the learned model. However, there are challenges to automatic text normalization. Natural language is by nature evolving, *e.g.* Urban Dictionary[1] is a crowdsourced online dictionary for slang words and phrases not typically found in a standard dictionary, but used in an informal setting such as text messages or social media posts. Moreover, abbreviations and emojis allow humans to express rich and informative content with few characters, but troubles machine understanding. Finally, humans are prone to spelling errors while writing or typing.

Due to the reasons mentioned above, developers have designed pre-processing techniques to normalise textual data, including spell correction, tokenisation, stemming, lemmatization and part-of-speech tagging. During the years, multiple libraries have been proposed to facilitate such pre-processing steps: *e.g.* NLTK (Bird, 2006), spaCy[2] or Stanford Core NLP (Manning et al., 2014). However, as textual domains vary greatly from medical records, legal documents to social media posts, there is no single solution or a fixed set of pre-processing steps for text normalization. Thus, up to date, defining a pre-processing pipeline remains an art form which requires a significant engineering effort. While researchers can define hard-policies to eliminate all noisy textual data, they also considerably reduce the amount of information available to the model, thus limit its performance. Such pruning approach appears problematic in the industry where engineers tackle domain-specific problems are given a relatively limited noisy textual dataset.

Enterprises also have to comply with multiple policies concerning privacy. Thus, they are re-

[1] https://www.urbandictionary.com/
[2] https://spacy.io/

Proceedings of the First Workshop on Natural Language Interfaces, pages 37–47
July 10, 2020. ©2020 Association for Computational Linguistics
https://doi.org/10.18653/v1/P17

Table 1: Example of well formatted text correctly masked with simple regex rules. Note that all the reported credit card number are artificially generated.

Unmasked Text	Masked Text
i need to delete my credit card 5496-9579-4394-2954	i need to delete my credit card ****
the refund will post to your credit card ending in (8077) in the next 3-5 business days	the refund will post to your credit card ending in (****) in the next 3-5 business days

Table 2: Examples of text over-masked due to regex application.

Over-Masked Text	Missing Information
I sent the faulty product back and provided PayPal with the tracking *********************** USPS.	Tracking Number
I was charged a fee for a payment from my son. He owed me *** and I only received 145.90. Can you please refund that fee to my account? Thank you	Money Amount

quired to mask or remove sensitive information rather than cache them inside data centers. Such sensitive information includes credit card numbers, email addresses and Social Security Number (SSN). Note that sanitation issues not only arise during an offline storage/backup process of user-generated content, but they might also happen in real-time. For example, it is common for big enterprises to outsource customer services, like live-chat or chat-bot systems, to third parties. Thus, there is the need to remove all the sensitive information before expose the input text to any third party to prevent information leakage. At the same time, the semantic meaning of a customer's request has to be preserved to deliver good customer support. Enterprises have traditionally addressed sanitization by defining heuristics. Such an approach is effective over well-defined text such as official documents and notes. As shown in Tab. 1, carefully designed regex rules are able to properly mask content following a specific pattern, *e.g.* credit card numbers, from a document[3]. Instead, in an informal setting regex rules can fail due to the presence of typos or sensitive information whose syntax is not accounted in the predefined patterns; for example:

- "my card ending -4810 has being refused."
- "i want to cancel my last transaction 6 9 0 8 2 0 5 7 3 D 1 4 8 0 4 3 3."

On the other hand, rules-based approaches, begin semantic-unaware, tend to mask most of the insensitive but crucial numerical information, troubling the downstream analysis. For instance, Tab. 2 demonstrates a case when a tracking number is confused with a transaction number. Similarly, in the second case, a transaction amount is confused with a credit card number.

As mentioned, we claim that it is not possible to define a general heuristics that correctly cover all the corner cases while ignoring semantics. Instead, we propose a novel approach for text normalization and sanitization based on the recent advancements made in NLP, specifically in Machine Translation (MT). That is, we formulate the joint text normalization and sanitization task as *learning to translate from non-canonical English to a sequence of well-defined or masked tokens*. For example, Tab. 3 demonstrates how malformed texts are translated into a semantically equivalent sequence of well-defined tokens with properly masked information. To our knowledge, this is the first attempt to formulate the joint text normalization and sanitization under MT framework. In so doing, we propose a novel network architecture for MT that can solve this multi-task learning problem.

Moreover, we address the thorny problem of generating unseen tokens during inference in sequence-to-sequence (seq2seq) learning by making use of pointer networks (Vinyals et al., 2015; See et al., 2017; Merity et al., 2016). In addition to the generator, we integrate the *pointer network*, a module that learns to directly copy a specific segment within the input text to the output sequence. Compare to previous work, our design of the pointer is novel as it learns to predict the start and end positions of the correct text segment to be copied, and is built upon the concept of multi-head attention and positional encoding (Vaswani et al., 2017). Experiments show that using a generating-pointing

[3]Note that all the personal information have been anonimized.

mechanism improves normalization performance compared to a pure generating mechanism. Our model can correctly identify and preserve most named entities contained in the input text, potentially benefits downstream analysis.

2 Related Work

The introduction of word embeddings (Hinton et al., 1986; Mikolov et al., 2013; Goldberg and Levy, 2014) has produced a gigantic leap forward for most NLP-related task. Traditional problems such as vector sparsity and word interaction were solved by a simple, yet effective, methodology that exploits a large corpus rather than a sophisticated algorithm. However, such methods are limited by the challenge of inferring embeddings for words unobserved at training time, *i.e.* Out-Of-Vocabulary (OOV). Such scenarios are common in many social-media related applications where the input text is generated in real-time. Thus, the user's malformed language might affect downstream performance (Hutto and Gilbert, 2014). Another solution is to include all the misspelling words in the training dataset or to impose similar embeddings for all n-character variations of a canonical word. This, would not scale well due to the sheer amount of such non-canonical terms; thus researchers have studied the spelling correction problem since long time (Church and Gale, 1991; Brill and Moore, 2000). However, traditional approaches are based on a word-per-word basis; which has shown acceptable results when applied to formal languages.

There have been many robust approaches to token-level spelling correction and lemmatization. The pioneering work done by Han and Baldwin demonstrated that micro-phonetic similarity could provide valuable insight to correct the spelling in an informal context, as many of these relaxed spellings are often based on the word's phonetic, *e.g thr* for *there* or *d* for *the*. Monoise (van der Goot, 2019a) generates feature-engineered n-character candidates for a misspelt word not found in the vocabulary and ranks them using a Random Forest Classifier. However, to accurately identify misspelt words, let alone normalizing them, optimal approaches need to consider the whole contextual semantics rather than the word-level morphology. For example, the utterance *Can I speak to a reel person?* is not misspelt at word-level as every word is a valid English word. However, if we consider sentence-level semantics, *reel* should be normalized into *real*. To factor in such contextual signals, recent advancements in NLP has considered these sequential nature of a written language as well as the long-term dependencies present in sentences. Thus, the research community has proposed different methodologies to perform micro-text normalisation based on deep learning (Min and Mott, 2015; Edizel et al., 2019; Gu et al., 2019; Satapathy et al., 2019). While we address the problem of text normalisation in the NLP context, it has also been adopted as a key component for speech applications (Sproat and Jaitly, 2016; Zhang et al., 2019).

Pointer Network was first proposed to solve geometric problems where the size of the output classes is a variable not conforming to the fixed multi-label classification of traditional seq2seq learning (Vinyals et al., 2015). Pointer Network becomes widely adopted in many NLP tasks including machine translation (Gulcehre et al., 2016), abstractive summarization (See et al., 2017) and language modeling (Merity et al., 2016) as it aids accurate reproduction of factual details such as unseen proper nouns commonly treated as OOVs. However, existing works formulate the pointing operation as a single position classification task that returns one word (token) position in the encoding sequence to be copied to the decoding sequence. Such formulation is no longer suitable for our char-to-word strategy. Furthermore, with the recent state-of-the-art in seq2seq learning introduced by the Transformer architecture, there has not been a comprehensive comparison between different attention strategies, *i.e.* the classical attention mechanisms (Luong et al., 2015) and multi-head attention (Vaswani et al., 2017) on this pointing objective.

Finally, none of the previous research considered the joint privacy-preserving issue, which is common in commercial NLIs such as virtual agents for customer services. To the best of our knowledge, (Sánchez et al., 2012) is the first model that attempted to solve the sanitization problem at a semantic level, without using a rule-based approach (Sweeney, 1996). However, the former approaches are based on manually defined policies that are application and context-specific or are limited to named entities; thus are not generalizable across domains and applications.

Table 3: Example of malformed input text is normalized in the output. Note that the tracking number is mapped to an unknown token while the transaction id is masked for security/privacy reasons.

Input Text	Output Text
D show jst gettin started.	the show is just getting started .
R u thr ?	are you there ?
Why it is my transaction with id 781243692BSD0433 on hold ?	why it is my transaction whith id <msk> on hold ?
I can't enter the tracking number 781243692BSD0433 for a refund.	i can not enter the tracking number <unk> for a refund

3 Problem Formulation

Neural seq2seq models (Sutskever et al., 2014; Cho et al., 2014; Vaswani et al., 2017) became the de facto standard for machine translation systems. Such models are composed by an encoder-decoder architecture which takes an input sequence $\mathbf{x} = [\mathrm{x}_1, ..., \mathrm{x}_M]$ and generate the desired output sequence $\mathbf{y} = [\mathrm{y}_1, ..., \mathrm{y}_N]$ according to the conditional probability distribution $P_\theta^{\text{gen}}(\mathbf{y}|\mathbf{x})$, where θ stands for the model parameters. Due to their well-designed factorisation of $P_\theta^{\text{gen}}(\mathbf{y}|\mathbf{x})$ based on an autoregressive approach:

$$P_\theta^{\text{gen}}(\mathbf{y}|\mathbf{x}) = \prod_{t=1}^{N} P_\theta(\mathrm{y}_t|\mathrm{y}_{t-1}, ..., \mathrm{y}_1, \mathbf{x}). \quad (1)$$

seq2seq models have been proven capable of solving the translation task with outstanding results. However, in the traditional MT settings $\mathbf{x}$ and $\mathbf{y}$ are tokens' sequences of different languages, instead, in our context $\mathbf{y}$ represents the same input sentence, but rewritten in a formal and anonymised language.

In addition to the next token generation objective, we formulate the pointing objective as outputting two sequences of start positions $\mathbf{u}^s = [\mathrm{u}_1^s, ..., \mathrm{u}_N^s]$ and end positions $\mathbf{u}^e = [\mathrm{u}_1^e, ..., \mathrm{u}_N^e]$ of the input encoding sequence where $\mathrm{u}_i^s, \mathrm{u}_i^e \in [1, ..., M-1]$. Similar to $\mathbf{y}$, $\mathbf{u}^s$ and $\mathbf{u}^e$ are chosen according to the conditional probability distributions $P_\theta^{\text{pt-start}}(\mathbf{u}|\mathbf{x})$ and $P_\theta^{\text{pt-end}}(\mathbf{u}|\mathbf{x})$ which can be factored as:

$$P_\theta^{\text{pt-start}}(\mathbf{u}^e|\mathbf{x}) = \prod_{t=1}^{N} P_\theta^{\text{pt-start}}(\mathrm{u}_t^s|\mathrm{y}_{t-1}, ..., \mathrm{y}_1, \mathbf{x}), \quad (2)$$

$$P_\theta^{\text{pt-end}}(\mathbf{u}^s|\mathbf{x}) = \prod_{t=1}^{N} P_\theta^{\text{pt-end}}(\mathrm{u}_t^e|\mathrm{y}_{t-1}, ..., \mathrm{y}_1, \mathbf{x}). \quad (3)$$

Note that the factorisation proposed in Eq. 2 (and 3), convert the intractable estimation of $\mathbf{u}^s$ conditioned on $\mathbf{x}$ in a sequence of classification tasks over the sequence length (M) predicting u_t^s based on the previous predictions $\mathrm{y}_{<t}$.

Finally, we learn the optimal θ by maximizing the joint likelihood of the distribution for generative normalisation and sanitisation, $P_\theta^{\text{gen}}(\mathbf{y}|\mathbf{x})$, and the distribution for pointing to the start and end positions for normalisation, $P_\theta^{\text{pt-start}}(\mathbf{u}^s|\mathbf{x})$, $P_\theta^{\text{pt-end}}(\mathbf{u}^e|\mathbf{x})$. In other words, our optimisation problem is the minimization of the well-known cross-entropy loss:

$$\begin{aligned} \theta^* = \underset{\theta}{\operatorname{argmin}} - \sum_{t=1}^{T} \Big[& \hat{\mathrm{y}}_t \log P_\theta^{\text{gen}}(\mathrm{y}_t|\mathrm{y}_{<t}, \mathbf{x}) \\ & + \hat{\mathrm{u}}_t^s \log P_\theta^{\text{pt-start}}(\mathrm{u}_t^s|\mathrm{y}_{<t}, \mathbf{x}) \\ & + \hat{\mathrm{u}}_t^e \log P_\theta^{\text{pt-end}}(\mathrm{u}_t^e|\mathrm{y}_{<t}, \mathbf{x}) \Big]. \end{aligned} \quad (4)$$

4 Proposed Method

4.1 Generator

It is possible to formalise the text normalisation task as a seq2seq problem, where malformed English is *translated* in well-defined English. In literature seq2seq (Sutskever et al., 2014) models and the similar Memory Networks (Gulcehre et al., 2017; Weston et al., 2014; Graves et al., 2014) have been widely applied to multiple tasks such as machine translation (Vaswani et al., 2017; Cho et al., 2014) , language inference (Sukhbaatar et al., 2015; Devlin et al., 2018; Dai et al., 2019), question answering (Devlin et al., 2018; Yang et al., 2019) and more. Still, in most cases, the model is expected to serve at a single granularity level: *i.e.* sequence of words to sequence of words (W2W), char-to-char (C2C) or subword-to-subword (Sw2Sw). While this guarantees consistency, these approaches are not suitable for our application. On the one hand, the limited vocabulary size is the main advantage of a C2C approach, but it is more computationally expensive and might generate misspelt words.

On the other hand, a W2W setting is affected by the huge vocabulary size and by the OOV problem, but it guarantees grammatically correct words. Thus, we propose to use a char-to-word (C2V) strategy, where the input sequence is handled as a string of characters, but the output is generated as a distribution over well-formed words. Such a design

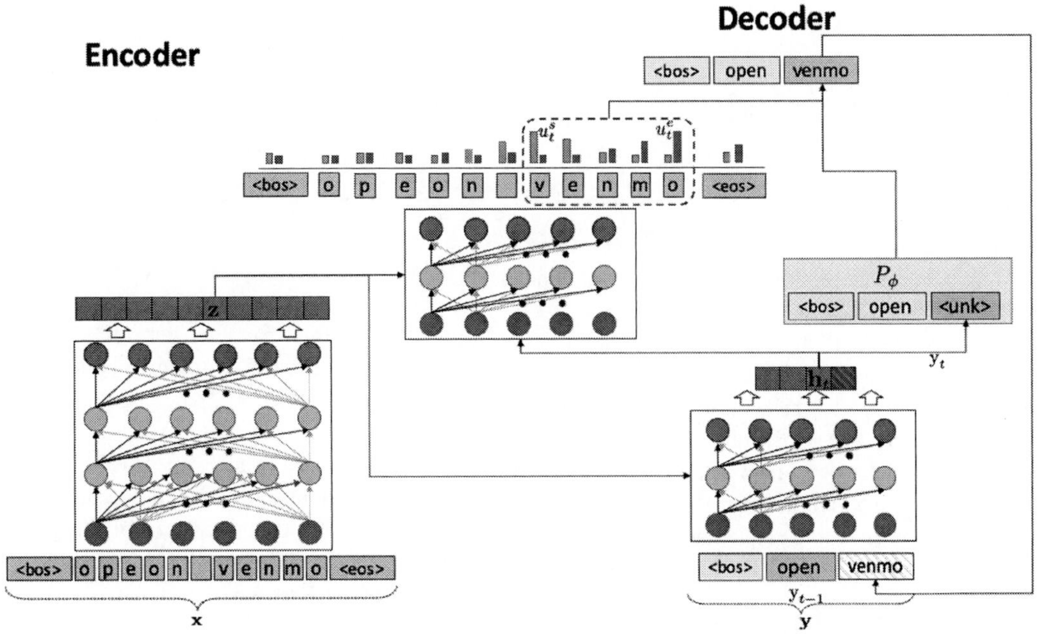

Figure 1: Model architecture. The left part represent a bidirectional encode based on the Transformer architectuGre, while the right part represent an auto-regressive decoder with pointing capabilities also based on the Transformer architecture. Note that, for each decoder timestep, the probabilities of the ith position in the encoder being the start and end positions are calculated from the **start** and **end** pointer distribution. The pointer and vocabulary distribution are derived from the **encoder hidden states** of the input text and **decoder hidden states** of the partial output text.

enables us to handle any input string, solving the problems related to spelling errors while certifying well-formed output. However, it imposes also some challenges; *e.g* how to embed conceptually different objects in the same low dimensional space, or how to learn time dependencies inside a long sequence of characters are only the major problems.

As shown in Fig. 1, given the input embedding of a sequence of characters $\mathbf{x} = [\mathrm{x}_1, ..., \mathrm{x}_M]$, we can formally define an encoder as:

$$\mathbf{q}, \mathbf{k}, \mathbf{v} = \mathbf{x}\mathbf{W}^{\mathrm{q}}, \mathbf{x}\mathbf{W}^{\mathrm{k}}, \mathbf{x}\mathbf{W}^{\mathrm{v}}, \tag{5}$$

$$\mathbf{z} = f(\mathbf{q}, \mathbf{k}, \mathbf{v}) \tag{6}$$

where $f(\cdot)$ is a bidirectional Transformer as defined in (Devlin et al., 2018). Similarly, given the output embedding of a sequence of words $\mathbf{y} = [\mathrm{y}_1, ..., \mathrm{y}_N]$ the decoder is defined as:

$$\mathbf{q}', \mathbf{k}', \mathbf{v}' = \mathbf{y}\mathbf{W}'^{\mathrm{q}}, \mathbf{y}\mathbf{W}'^{\mathrm{k}}, \mathbf{y}\mathbf{W}'^{\mathrm{v}}, \tag{7}$$

$$\mathbf{h}_t = f'(\mathbf{q}', \mathbf{k}', \mathbf{v}', \mathbf{z}) \tag{8}$$

where $f'(\cdot)$ is a traditional Transformer decoder applied in an auto-regressive settings as in (Vaswani et al., 2017). Note that, we are differentiate from the original implementation as we adopt a C2W approach.

4.2 Pointer

We address the limitation of generating unseen tokens in our design of the pointer network. As our generator module predicts a token from a fixed dictionary (vocabulary), it fails to normalise OOVs. We add a *pointer* module to our neural network that allows it to copy a segment of the input text if an unknown word is detected. Although previous works designed their pointer module to point to a single position, for our char-to-word learning problem where each position indicates a character, we propose to jointly point to a start and an end position, while coping all characters in-between. As the output token often consists of consecutive characters, this strategy effectively avoids copying a long continuous character sequence over multiple steps.

Formally, at the decoder timestep t, we learn to output the start position u_t^s and end position u_t^e by maximisation of Eq. 2 and Eq. 3 respectively. The pointer distribution for the start position is a function of the encoder representation $\mathbf{z}$ and the decoder representation $\mathbf{h}_t$ at t, or $P_\theta^{\text{pt-start}}(\mathrm{u}_t^s|\mathrm{y}_{<t}, \mathbf{x}) = g^s(\mathbf{h}_t, \mathbf{z})$. Given that, we can formally define the attention mechanism of the

Transformer architecture as:

$$\text{attn}_i(\mathbf{q}, \mathbf{k}) = \text{softmax}(\frac{\mathbf{q}_i \cdot \mathbf{k}_i^T}{\sqrt{d_K}}), \tag{9}$$

$$\mathbf{z} = [\text{attn}_0(\mathbf{q}, \mathbf{k}), ..., \text{attn}_N(\mathbf{q}, \mathbf{k})]\mathbf{W}^O \tag{10}$$

where d_K stands for the output dimension of $\mathbf{W}^\mathbf{k}$, $[\cdot, ..., \cdot]$ is the concatenation of N different attention heads and $\mathbf{W}^O$ is a linear transformation.

Our pointer distribution can be formulated as the attention probability of the last decoder hidden state at timestep t towards each position of the encoder hidden state $\mathbf{z}$. Specifically, we treat $\mathbf{h}_t$ as the query vector $\mathbf{q}$; while $\mathbf{z}$ is the key sequence $\mathbf{k}$ in Eq. 10. We derive the probability of the i-th position of the encoding sequence being the start position as:

$$g_i^s(\mathbf{h}_t, \mathbf{z}) = [\text{attn}_0(\mathbf{h}_t, \mathbf{z}), ..., \text{attn}_N(\mathbf{h}_t, \mathbf{z})]_i \mathbf{W}^s.$$

Notice that unlike the original multihead attention, we did not concern about the value sequence $\mathbf{v}$, but we directly use the attention output to detect the pointing position. Similarly, we define the probability of the j-th position being the end position to copy as:

$$g_j^e(\mathbf{h}_t, \mathbf{z}) = [\text{attn}_0(\mathbf{h}_t, \mathbf{z}), ..., \text{attn}_N(\mathbf{h}_t, \mathbf{z})]_j \mathbf{W}^e.$$

5 Experiments

We conducted 3 experiments to verify the effectiveness of our proposed model. 1) For improved joint normalization and sanitization, we compare our context-aware model with: 1.1) a traditional token-level lemmatizer and spelling corrector, and 1.2) a LSTM W2W encoder-decoder model. 2) For improved normalization of proper nouns, we compare our multi-head attentional pointer-generator with 2.1) a generator-only and a pointer-only baseline, and 2.2) the traditional attention encoder-decoder model. 3) Finally, to address the utility of text normalization we evaluate the performance's improvement obtained on a text classification task with or without text normalization.

The seq2seq transformer architecture we used has 4 attention heads and 5 layers with 100 hidden units. The maximum number input characters and output words are 600 and 300 respectively. During evaluation we maintain a beam size of 3. We determine the correct positions for the pointer network by matching any output word to its character list if the characters appear consecutively in the input character sequence, and noting the start and end position of that character list. Words whose characters are not found consecutively are assign a start and end position of 0 (the beginning of the sequence). We fix the start and end position to the nearest left and right space respectively in the input character sequence to select a complete word. We use the pointer output instead of the generator output whenever the predicted probability for generation is less than 0.6.

Table 4: The datasets' statistics used for evaluation.

	Conversational	Classification
Total size	66151	17851
Training Set	54110	6851
Validation Set	6020	5500
Test Set	6021	5500

5.1 Datasets

We conducted the experiments on two datasets:

• The former dataset contains conversations occurred between a customer and a live-chat agent. Human annotators provide the normalized and sanitized version as ground turth. We will refer to this as the *Conversational* dataset and use it for the evaluation of the first two experiments.

• The later one contains utterances collected from a task-oriented chatbot service where customers interact with an agent to solve 27 possible tasks. Each utterance has been manually inspected and assigned to one of the possible class. We will refer to this as the *Classification* datasets and we will adopt it for the last experiments in Sec. 6.3.

We report the dataset statistics in Tab. 4 and the detailed descriptions in Sec. 8.1.

5.2 Baselines

We adopted two baselines to benchmark the ability of the proposed model in the task of normalizing and sanitizing a sentence. The first baseline, Monoise (van der Goot, 2019b) – a lexical normalization tool, is adopted to confirm our model's effectiveness over token-based approaches. Monoise performs normalization via two subtasks: *candidate generation* and *candidate ranking*. The first subtask uses heuristics to select potential normalized forms of each token, including nearest neighbors in word embedding space, edit distance and phonetic distance, and crafted lookup list derived from training, and more. The second subtask first

Table 5: Performance of our proposed Transformer versus baseline in text normalization and sanitization.

Systems	Normalization		Sanitization	
	BLEU4	WER	BLEU4	WER
Monoise	0.9536	0.0206	-	-
LSTM	0.9955	0.0015	0.9827	0.0076
Transformer (Our model)	**0.9986**	**0.0007**	**0.9880**	**0.0052**

engineers features for each candidate, including word embedding distance, n-gram probability, character order, and more. This baseline is used to demonstrate the improvement of our approaches over a heuristic token-based model not only in terms of effectiveness but also efficiency.

The second baseline, LSTM implemented using Fairseq (Ott et al., 2019), is used to highlight the effectiveness of our char-to-word Transformer-based proposal over traditional word-to-word RNN.

Based on the previous research done in the MT filed, we report the test performances of normalization and sanitization in terms of BLEU4 and Word Error Rate (Klakow and Peters, 2002) (WER). The experiment results are described in Tab. 5.

We also (2.1) compare the performance of our proposed pointer-generator model against generator-only model in text normalisation objective and, (2.2) compare multi-head attention against classical attention mechanisms described in a previous work (Luong et al., 2015). The alternative attention formulation considered for benchmarking are:

- **General attention**

$$g_i^s(\mathbf{h}_t, \mathbf{z}, \theta_s) = \mathbf{h}_t^T W_s \mathbf{z}_i$$
$$g_i^e(\mathbf{h}_t, \mathbf{z}, \theta_e) = \mathbf{h}_t^T W_e \mathbf{z}_i$$

- **Concat attention**

$$g_i^s(\mathbf{h}_t, \mathbf{z}, \theta_s) = v_s^T \tanh(W_s[\mathbf{h}_t^T, \mathbf{z}_i])$$
$$g_i^e(\mathbf{h}_t, \mathbf{z}, \theta_s) = v_e^T \tanh(W_e[\mathbf{h}_t^T, \mathbf{z}_i]).$$

Note that, for an overall comparison of the different network architectures considered we used the BLEU4 score. Instead, to evaluate the pointing mechanisms, we compute the accuracy score of the start and end position w.r.t. the correct text's segment, as well as the improved F_1 score of the proposed model and baselines. The experiment results are described in Tab. 7.

Finally, the classification is done using a linear classifier with a bag-of-word approach; which is a common settings in the industry. The performance are evaluated in terms of accuracy and F_1 score. The results are reported in Tab. 9.

6 Results and Evaluation

6.1 Generator

At the macro-scopic level, all translation models, *i.e.* LSTM and the proposed Transformer-based out-perform Monoise. Specifically, our model outperforms Monoise by 0.045 absolute margin or reduces the error by 33 times in terms of BLEU4 score. In terms of WER, the result is performance is consistent where our model reduces the error by 0.02 or by 29 times. Overall, this highlights the improvement of context-aware translation models from context-unaware token-based lemmatizers. We also highlight the superiority of our Transformer-based architecture over the RNN baseline. On normalization task, it is able to reduce LSTM's error by approximately 3 times in terms of BLEU4 and 2 times in terms of WER. On Sanitization task, the proposed model consistently reduces LSTM's error by approximately 1.5 times in terms of both BLEU4 and WER.

For a deeper understanding of the models behavior, we examine the results at micro-scopic level in Tab. 6. We observe that in the first example, Monoise, being unaware of the context, normalize *shipping address* to *ship address*. This can be confusing as the phrase *shipping address* specifically means the delivery address of a package, while *ship address* possibly means the docking location of a large watercraft. Instead, the proposed model is able to consider the contextual information such as *my order*, indicating a package to be delivered, and leave the word *shipping* as it is. In the second example, Monoise leaves the word *real* unlemmatized as *reel* is an existing English word. However, when we factor in the context of virtual agent and the followed word *person*, normalizing *reel* as *real* is more sensible. Overall, also the analysis of the last example demonstrate how the proposed model is able to consider the semantics of an utterance; which eventualy lead to a better results w.r.t. a token-based approach.

6.2 Pointer

As shown in Tab. 7, all the networks with pointing capabilities outperform the Generator-only baseline in terms of BLEU score. Multihead Pointer-Generator improves Generator-only model by the

Table 6: Test examples highlight the behaviours of different methods. Note that, misspelled phrases are highlighted in red and correctly normalised phrases are highlighted in **blue**.

Input Text	Transformer (Our model)	Monoise
shipping address is incorrect on my order.	shipping address is incorrect on my order .	ship address is incorrect on my order .
can i speak with a reel person?	can i speak with a **real** person ?	can i speak with a reel person ?
i had money that was refunded to me and i tried sending to my bank account but its was on hold	i have money that was refund to me and i try send it to my bank account but **it was** on hold	i have money that was refund to me and i try send it to my bank account but it is was on hold

Table 7: Performance of our proposed Multihead Pointer-Generator versus baselines in text normalisation. The *Pointer Start Acc.* and *Pointer End Acc.* denote the accuracy of each system in pointing to the correct start and end position. The *Generating* F_1 denotes the F_1 score of each system in generating the correct next token.

Systems	BLEU4	Pointer Start Acc.	Pointer End Acc.	Generating F_1
Generator-only	0.9532	–	–	0.9243
General Pointer-Generator	0.9583	0.7083	0.7084	0.9229
Concat Pointer-Generator	0.9582	0.707	0.7065	0.928
Multihead Pointer-Generator	**0.9606**	0.7076	0.7076	**0.9334**

Table 8: Test examples highlight the behaviours of different methods.Note that: misspelled phrases are highlighted in red, correctly normalised phrases are highlighted in **blue**, mishandled OOVs are highlighted in gray, and, correctly pointed OOVs are highlighted in green.

Input Text	Generator-only Output	Pointer-only Ouput	Pointer-Generator Output
sennd mony from PayPal to venmo account	**send money** from PayPal to UNK account .	sennd mony from PayPal to venmo account .	**send money** from PayPal to venmo account .
how can I conect my venmo account with hsbc and citibank account?	how can i **connect** my UNK account with hub and UNK account ?	how can i conect my venmo account with hsbc and citibank account ?	how can i **connect** my venmo account with hsbc and citibank account ?
followw PayPal on twitter	**follow PayPal** on UNK .	followw PayPal on twitter .	**follow PayPal** on twitter .

largest absolute margin of .0074 or 15.8% error reduction, compared with .0061 absolute margin or 10.89% error reduction and 0.006 absolute margin or 10.68% error reduction from General and Concat Pointer-Generator respectively. These statics confirm our hypothesis that jointly using a pointing and generating mechanism improves the performance of neural models. Moreover, our Multihead Pointer-Generator being highly compatible with the end-to-end transformer-based architecture is the most effective amongst the proposed pointer-based models.

We further seek to understand the improvement brought about by our proposed Multihead Pointer-Generator by examining its accuracy in pointing to the correct start and end positions of the text segment to be copied. Experiment results from *Pointer Start Acc.* and *Pointer End Acc.* Table 8 suggest that there is no significant difference in pointing to the correct positions between the three pointer models. However, the Multihead Pointer-Generator shows a performance boost in terms of F_1 score, where our proposed model enhances the Generator baseline by 0.0091 absolute margin or 12.02% error reduction. This is significantly higher than the changes brought about by General (+1.84% error), and Concat (+4.89% error). This implies that our network design is capable of enhancing a traditional *Generator*-only module when applied to the text normalisation tasks.

Table 9: Classification performances with and without text normalized and sanitized input.

Systems	Accuracy	F_1 score
with text-norm	0.7696	0.7175
without text-norm.	0.7583	0.6855

6.3 Classification

Finally, we want to evaluate if text normalization and sanitization is also beneficial for downstream tasks. That is, we hypothesized that a normalized and sanitized utterance would be easier to process by another model such as a text classifier. Recent advancement in NLP claims that BERT-like models can easily overcome limitations related to misspelling errors due to their tokenization and pre-training process. However, such models are computational expensive thus are not yet widely adopted in commercial applications that require high-throughput like chatbot services.

It has to be noted that our Conversational dataset contains a broader set of topics and a more variegate lexicon than this dataset. Thus, for this experiment, we directly apply the best performing model of task 1 and 2 to obtain a normalized and sanitized version of the input utterances.

Tab. 9 reports the impact of text normalization and sanitization on a downstream text classification task in our NLI that requires strong natural language understanding. Overall, our proposed model yields a relative improvement of $+1.08\%$ in terms of accuracy and $+4.67\%$ in terms of F_1 score. This indicates that text normalization is beneficial in detecting the classes characterized by a limited amount of training examples.

7 Conclusion

We addressed the importance of context awareness in joint normalization and sanitization. We verified our C2W Transformer-based model's quality over context-unaware word-level lemmatizer and traditional W2W seq-to-seq model at both macroscopic and microscopic level. Moreover, we tackled the limitation of representing and producing OOVs during generation with a pointer-generator that learns to copy the relevant text segments from the source input to the translated output. Experiments at both macroscopic and microscopic level verified improved normalization and sanitization fluency previously limited by OOVs.

Our formulation of text normalization as a learning-to-translate problem avoids the tedious engineering of domain specific preprocessing heuristics for textual data. The proposal of pointer-generator is highly generalizable to other NLP tasks such as summarization or machine translation.

References

Steven Bird. 2006. NLTK: The Natural Language Toolkit. In *Proceedings of the COLING/ACL 2006 Interactive Presentation Sessions*, pages 69–72, Sydney, Australia. Association for Computational Linguistics.

Eric Brill and Robert C Moore. 2000. An improved error model for noisy channel spelling correction. In *Proceedings of the 38th Annual Meeting on Association for Computational Linguistics*, pages 286–293. Association for Computational Linguistics.

Kyunghyun Cho, Bart Van Merriënboer, Caglar Gulcehre, Dzmitry Bahdanau, Fethi Bougares, Holger Schwenk, and Yoshua Bengio. 2014. Learning phrase representations using rnn encoder-decoder for statistical machine translation. *arXiv preprint arXiv:1406.1078*.

Kenneth W Church and William A Gale. 1991. Probability scoring for spelling correction. *Statistics and Computing*, 1(2):93–103.

Zihang Dai, Zhilin Yang, Yiming Yang, William W Cohen, Jaime Carbonell, Quoc V Le, and Ruslan Salakhutdinov. 2019. Transformer-xl: Attentive language models beyond a fixed-length context. *arXiv preprint arXiv:1901.02860*.

Jacob Devlin, Ming-Wei Chang, Kenton Lee, and Kristina Toutanova. 2018. Bert: Pre-training of deep bidirectional transformers for language understanding. *arXiv preprint arXiv:1810.04805*.

Bora Edizel, Aleksandra Piktus, Piotr Bojanowski, Rui Ferreira, Edouard Grave, and Fabrizio Silvestri. 2019. Misspelling oblivious word embeddings. *arXiv preprint arXiv:1905.09755*.

Yoav Goldberg and Omer Levy. 2014. word2vec explained: deriving mikolov et al.'s negative-sampling word-embedding method. *arXiv preprint arXiv:1402.3722*.

Rob van der Goot. 2019a. Monoise: A multi-lingual and easy-to-use lexical normalization tool. In *Proceedings of the 57th Annual Meeting of the Association for Computational Linguistics: System Demonstrations*, pages 201–206.

Rob van der Goot. 2019b. MoNoise: A multi-lingual and easy-to-use lexical normalization tool. In *Proceedings of the 57th Annual Meeting of the Association for Computational Linguistics: System Demonstrations*, pages 201–206, Florence, Italy. Association for Computational Linguistics.

Alex Graves, Greg Wayne, and Ivo Danihelka. 2014. Neural turing machines. *arXiv preprint arXiv:1410.5401*.

Jiatao Gu, Changhan Wang, and Jake Zhao. 2019. Levenshtein transformer. *arXiv preprint arXiv:1905.11006*.

Caglar Gulcehre, Sungjin Ahn, Ramesh Nallapati, Bowen Zhou, and Yoshua Bengio. 2016. Pointing the unknown words. *arXiv preprint arXiv:1603.08148*.

Caglar Gulcehre, Sarath Chandar, and Yoshua Bengio. 2017. Memory augmented neural networks with wormhole connections. *arXiv preprint arXiv:1701.08718*.

Isabelle Guyon, Nada Matic, Vladimir Vapnik, et al. 1996. Discovering informative patterns and data cleaning.

Bo Han and Timothy Baldwin. 2011. Lexical normalisation of short text messages: Makn sens a# twitter. In *Proceedings of the 49th Annual Meeting of the Association for Computational Linguistics: Human Language Technologies-Volume 1*, pages 368–378. Association for Computational Linguistics.

Geoffrey E Hinton et al. 1986. Learning distributed representations of concepts. In *Proceedings of the eighth annual conference of the cognitive science society*, volume 1, page 12. Amherst, MA.

Clayton J Hutto and Eric Gilbert. 2014. Vader: A parsimonious rule-based model for sentiment analysis of social media text. In *Eighth international AAAI conference on weblogs and social media*.

Dietrich Klakow and Jochen Peters. 2002. Testing the correlation of word error rate and perplexity. *Speech Communication*, 38(1-2):19–28.

Thang Luong, Hieu Pham, and Christopher D Manning. 2015. Effective approaches to attention-based neural machine translation. In *Proceedings of the 2015 Conference on Empirical Methods in Natural Language Processing*, pages 1412–1421.

Christopher D. Manning, Mihai Surdeanu, John Bauer, Jenny Finkel, Steven J. Bethard, and David McClosky. 2014. The Stanford CoreNLP natural language processing toolkit. In *Association for Computational Linguistics (ACL) System Demonstrations*, pages 55–60.

Stephen Merity, Caiming Xiong, James Bradbury, and Richard Socher. 2016. Pointer sentinel mixture models. *arXiv preprint arXiv:1609.07843*.

Tomas Mikolov, Ilya Sutskever, Kai Chen, Greg S Corrado, and Jeff Dean. 2013. Distributed representations of words and phrases and their compositionality. In *Advances in neural information processing systems*, pages 3111–3119.

Wookhee Min and Bradford Mott. 2015. Ncsu_sas_wookhee: a deep contextual long-short term memory model for text normalization. In *Proceedings of the Workshop on Noisy User-generated Text*, pages 111–119.

Myle Ott, Sergey Edunov, Alexei Baevski, Angela Fan, Sam Gross, Nathan Ng, David Grangier, and Michael Auli. 2019. fairseq: A fast, extensible toolkit for sequence modeling. In *Proceedings of NAACL-HLT 2019: Demonstrations*.

Erhard Rahm and Hong Hai Do. 2000. Data cleaning: Problems and current approaches. *IEEE Data Eng. Bull.*, 23(4):3–13.

David Sánchez, Montserrat Batet, and Alexandre Viejo. 2012. Detecting sensitive information from textual documents: an information-theoretic approach. In *International Conference on Modeling Decisions for Artificial Intelligence*, pages 173–184. Springer.

R. Satapathy, Y. Li, S. Cavallari, and E. Cambria. 2019. Seq2seq deep learning models for microtext normalization. In *2019 International Joint Conference on Neural Networks (IJCNN)*, pages 1–8.

Abigail See, Peter J Liu, and Christopher D Manning. 2017. Get to the point: Summarization with pointer-generator networks. In *Proceedings of the 55th Annual Meeting of the Association for Computational Linguistics (Volume 1: Long Papers)*, pages 1073–1083.

Richard Sproat and Navdeep Jaitly. 2016. Rnn approaches to text normalization: A challenge. *arXiv preprint arXiv:1611.00068*.

Sainbayar Sukhbaatar, Jason Weston, Rob Fergus, et al. 2015. End-to-end memory networks. In *Advances in neural information processing systems*, pages 2440–2448.

Ilya Sutskever, Oriol Vinyals, and Quoc V Le. 2014. Sequence to sequence learning with neural networks. In *Advances in neural information processing systems*, pages 3104–3112.

Latanya Sweeney. 1996. Replacing personally-identifying information in medical records, the scrub system. In *Proceedings of the AMIA annual fall symposium*, page 333. American Medical Informatics Association.

Ashish Vaswani, Noam Shazeer, Niki Parmar, Jakob Uszkoreit, Llion Jones, Aidan N Gomez, Łukasz Kaiser, and Illia Polosukhin. 2017. Attention is all you need. In *Advances in neural information processing systems*, pages 5998–6008.

Oriol Vinyals, Meire Fortunato, and Navdeep Jaitly. 2015. Pointer networks. In *Advances in Neural Information Processing Systems*, pages 2692–2700.

Jason Weston, Sumit Chopra, and Antoine Bordes. 2014. Memory networks. *arXiv preprint arXiv:1410.3916*.

Zhilin Yang, Zihang Dai, Yiming Yang, Jaime Carbonell, Ruslan Salakhutdinov, and Quoc V Le. 2019. Xlnet: Generalized autoregressive pretraining for language understanding. *arXiv preprint arXiv:1906.08237*.

Hao Zhang, Richard Sproat, Axel H Ng, Felix Stahlberg, Xiaochang Peng, Kyle Gorman, and Brian Roark. 2019. Neural models of text normalization for speech applications. *Computational Linguistics*, 45(2):293–337.

8 Appendix

8.1 Dataset Details

As described in Sec. 5.1, we adopted two distinct datasets in our evaluation. Here we are going to describe their characteristics and the annotation process used.

Conversational Dataset

As over-mentioned, this dataset is formed by utterances collected from a chat service where clients interact with customers service agents. Note that such conversations happen in real-time. Thus they contain a huge variety of topics as well as a huge lexicon. Clients can access this chat service from any device, this translate in many syntactic errors present in the utterances as well as an informal language. All the above considerations suggest that many customers adopt mobile devices to interact with these services. The topics covered in such conversations can vary from issues related to financial services to trust problem, which involves third parties not directly participating in the conversations or general chitchatting.

Human annotator has been used to reduce each word o its canonical form, *i.e.* lemmas. In contrast, misspelt words and sensitive/personal information are corrected or masked according to the contextual meaning of the conversation. Note that this labelling process contains little uncertainty; thus, we used a single annotator per utterance to maximise the dataset size.

Classification Dataset

The second dataset is a traditional text classification dataset collected from a task-oriented chatbot system where customers can interact with a chatbot agent to solve 27 possibles task. Note that the user interface is equal for both dataset, but in this case, instead of a human agent, there is a chatbot agent. It has to be noted that we collect only the first utterance typed from the customer since it is the only part needed to classify the customer's need on the 27 classes correctly.

3 skilled annotators have manually annotated each utterance, and we have discharged all the utterances that do not present 100% of agreement. The classes used in this dataset are a subset of the topics appearing in the previous dataset. For example, we have classes related to transactions status, transactions that are declined, dispute for item not received, scam emails or problems related to the account of a customer. Note that, if the chatbot is not able to address the customer's need the conversation would be redirected to an human agent. Thus, a system able to normalize and sanitize utterances from the live-chat service (Conversational dataset), would be directly applicable also to this dataset.

Author Index

Association for Computational Linguistics
209 N. Eighth Street
Stroudsburg, Pennsylvania 18360

ISBN 978-1-7138-1376-7

9 781713 813767